Hittin' the Trail

Day Hiking the St. Croix National Scenic Riverway

By Rob Bignell

Atiswinic Press · Ojai, Calif.

HITTIN' THE TRAIL: DAY HIKING
THE ST. CROIX NATIONAL SCENIC RIVERWAY

Copyright Rob Bignell, 2014

Atiswinic Press
Ojai, Calif. 93023
hikeswithtykes.com/hittinthetrail_home.html

ISBN 978-0-9896723-4-4
Library of Congress Control Number 2014936129

Cover design by Rob Bignell
Cover photo of St. Croix River near St. Croix Falls, Wis.

Manufactured in the United States of America
First printing April 2014

For Kieran
And two lifetimes of
adventure together!

Table of Contents

INTRODUCTION   1

The Scenic Riverway South to North   3
Attractions   5
Kid-Friendly Activities   6
How to Get There   8
When to Visit   10
Maps   10

ST. CROIX RIVER TRAILS   11
Carpenter St. Croix Valley
Nature Center   12
  South River Bluff Trail
St. Croix Bluffs Regional Park   14
  St. Croix Bluffs Trail
Kinnickinnic State Park   15
  Purple Trail
  Other Kinnickinnic State Park Trails
Afton State Park   19
  North River Trail
  Other Afton State Park Trails
Willow River State Park   22
  Hidden Ponds Nature (Black) Trail
  Burkhardt (Pink) Trail

Other Willow River State Park Trails
Stillwater Area Trails   27
Brown's Creek Park and Nature Preserve
   Ski Trail segment
St. Croix Boom Site Trail
William O'Brien State Park   30
Riverside Trail
Other William O'Brien State Park Trails
Osceola Area Trails   34
Cascade Falls Trail
Ridge View (Osceola and Chisago) Trails
**Osceola Bedrock Glades State
Natural Area**   38
Ridgeview Trail
Wisconsin Interstate State Park   41
Summit Rock Trail
Lake O' the Dalles Trail
Other Wisconsin Interstate State
   Park Trails
Minnesota Interstate State Park   46
Shadow and Angle Rocks Lookout Trail
Other Minnesota Interstate State Park Trails
St. Croix Falls Area Trails   49
Indianhead Flowage Trail
Other St. Croix Falls Area Trails
Wild River State Park   51
River Terrace Loop
Other Wild River State Park Trails
Grantsburg Area Trails   54
Sandrock Cliffs Trail

Governor Knowles State Forest　　56
Cedar Interpretive Trail
Other Governor Knowles State
　Forest Trails
Chengwatana State Forest　　60
Redhorse Creek Northern Loop
Other Chengwatana State Forest Trails
St. Croix State Park　　63
Kettle River Highbanks to Observation
　Tower Route
Other St. Croix State Park Trails
St. Croix State Forest　　65
Gandy Dancer State Trail segment
Other St. Croix State Forest Trails
Schoen/Louise Parks　　67
Schoen/Louise Parks Jeep Trail
**Buckley Creek Barrens State
Natural Area**　　69
Buckley Creek Barrens Trail
Gordon Dam County Park　　71
Gordon Flowage Campground Trail
Brule River State Forest　　73
Bois Brule-St. Croix River Historic
　Portage Trail

NAMEKAGON RIVER TRAILS　　77
Danbury Area Trails　　78
Namekagon Delta Trail
Trego Area Trails　　79
Trego Lake Trail

Trego Nature Trail
Wild Rivers Trail segment
Hayward Area Trails   84
Namekagon-Laccourt Oreilles Portage Trail
Cable Area Trails   86
Namekagon Dam Landing Trail

BEST TRAILS LIST   89

**BONUS SECTION: DAY HIKING
PRIMER**   93
Selecting a Trail   93
Clothing   96
Equipment   99
Navigational Tools   105
Food and Water   107
First-aid Kit   110
Hiking with Children: Attitude Adjustment   113
Family Dog   114
Rules of the Trail   115
Trail Dangers   118

INDEX   123

Introduction

I magine a land where you can walk through lush green forests and alongside crystal blue rivers...where you can lean against 200-year-old trees or feel the splash of hidden waterfalls ...where you can retrace the steps of historic portages or watch bald eagle families soar overhead. Such a place not only exists, it has been preserved for all to enjoy – it's called the St. Croix National Scenic Riverway.

Located along the Minnesota-Wisconsin border and across the latter's Northwoods, the scenic riverway includes most of the St. Croix River and all of the Namekagon River. The National Park Service runs the scenic riverway, but a patchwork of state and county parks, nonprofit nature centers, and state forests combine to protect 252 contiguous miles of the two waterways. A whole variety of recreational activities, from camping and fishing to canoeing and day hiking, await there.

Just a few hours' drive at most for anyone living in Minnesota, Wisconsin, northern Illinois, northeast Iowa, and Michigan's Upper Peninsula, the scenic riverway's proximity to the Minneapolis-St. Paul International Airport makes it easier to reach

than most national parks. Indeed, the scenic riverway outperforms attendance of more than half of all
national parks; annual attendance now tops
520,000 visitors.

The scenic riverway wouldn't exist at all if not for
a major geological event dating some 1.1 billion
years ago. At that time, massive lava flows covered
this part of the world. This basalt now forms a
strong bedrock that is the foundation of the St.
Croix River gorge, the surrounding landscape, and
Lake Superior to the north.

The sandstone above the basalt began forming
some 515 million years ago when this region sat
under a warm shallow sea near the equator. As
sediments piled up and were covered over the
eons, they hardened into rock; the landscape finally rose above the sea about 345 million years ago.

Then about 10,000 years ago at the end of the
last ice age, a glacial torrent swept through the
area when ancient Lake Duluth drained south. This
flood carved the St. Croix River valley and left
many intriguing cliff formations.

Since the last ice age, Native Americans have
used the St. Croix and Namekagon for trade and
travel. When European explorers and fur traders
arrived during the late 1600s, they mainly saw the
waterways as quick routes connecting the Great
Lakes to the Mississippi River; so vital was this link
that by 1688 the French had established Fort St.
Croix ("Fort Holy Cross") along the St. Croix, giv-

ing the river its modern name.

Throughout the 1700s, the river area was hotly contested, first by Ojibwe and Dakota Indians living there and then the French and the British.

Following the Revolutionary War, the United States wrested control of the area from the British but would not assert any real power over it until the 1830s when the Treaty of St. Peters was signed with the Ojibwe. This opened the area to logging, which dominated the two riverways and surrounding forests for the rest of the century. Many of today's towns along the rivers got their start thanks to the logging industry.

During the 20th century, the economy along the rivers shifted to agriculture, but with the growth of the nearby Minneapolis-St. Paul metro area, a number of conservationists and concerned citizens feared the riverway was ripe for commercial exploitation. Their efforts led to the National Wild and Scenic Rivers Act of 1968, which protected significant portions of the St. Croix and Namekagon north of Taylors Falls, Minn.

Just four years later, Congress protected the St. Croix south of Taylors Falls to Prescott, Wis., by creating the Lower St. Croix National Scenic Riverway.

The Scenic Riverway South to North

From south to north, the scenic riverway begins in Prescott, where the St. Croix River meets the

Mississippi River. This wide stretch of the St. Croix often is referred to as Lake St. Croix, which sports two state parks. At Afton, Minn., and Hudson, Wis., the Interstate 94 bridge handles the greatest amount of vehicle traffic over the river. Willow River State Park sits on a tributary to the St. Croix in what is Lake St. Croix's most populous stretch, with the cities of Bayport, Oak Park Heights and Stillwater on the Minnesota side and Hudson and North Hudson on the Wisconsin side.

North of Stillwater, the population falls off greatly, with William O'Brien State Park in Minnesota sometimes outpacing the census of the neighboring town, Marine on St. Croix. Then another cluster of villages appears – Osceola, Dresser and St. Croix Falls on the Wisconsin side and Taylors Falls in Minnesota. There the twin jewels of Minnesota and Wisconsin Interstate State Parks straddles the St. Croix O' the Dalles, a beautiful gorge that the river flows through.

North of this region, the river bulges westward, with a state park in Minnesota and several state forests and state natural areas on both sides, before curving eastward to Danbury, Wis. A few miles north of town, the river ceases to be the state border as it heads northeast, taking in the Namekagon, and then coming to the Saint Croix Flowage near Gordon, Wis. The scenic riverway ends at the dam creating the lake.

West of the flowage, the St. Croix continues

northward as a narrow waterway to its headwaters at Upper St. Croix Lake. In all, it's a 169-mile journey.

The St. Croix's largest tributary, the Namekagon, meanders for 101 miles, crossing four Wisconsin counties. It's a major recreational area, with a number of boat landings and campsites, especially in Sawyer and Washburn counties.

From west to east, the Namekagon dips south to Trego, Wis., before heading northeast through Hayward, Wis. Its headwaters are at Namakagon Lake in the Chequamegon National Forest. The tributary runs 101 miles.

Attractions

With the quiltwork of state parks, forests, and natural areas, county parks and other historical sites across the scenic riverway, attractions abound – swimming beaches, boat ramps, campgrounds, shopping in historic towns, ski trails, and more. Well over 70 day hiking trails can be found along the two rivers.

The National Park Service operates two visitor centers in the riverway. The St. Croix River Visitor Center is in downtown St. Croix Falls and open from mid-April to Oct. 27. It boasts a 500-gallon freshwater aquarium. The Namekagon River Visitor Center is a mile east of Trego and open from Memorial Day Weekend through Labor Day. Hours for both visitor centers are 9 a.m. to 5 p.m. daily.

Major parks, nature centers, and public forests on or near the scenic riverway (from south to north and west to east) include:

■ Carpenter St. Croix Valley Nature Center (Hastings, Minn.)

■ St. Croix Bluffs Regional Park (Hastings)

■ Kinnickinnic State Park (Prescott)

■ Afton State Park (Afton)

■ Willow River State Park (Hudson)

■ William O'Brien State Park (Marine on St. Croix)

■ Osceola Bedrock Glades State Natural Area (Osceola)

■ Wisconsin Interstate State Park (St. Croix Falls)

■ Minnesota Interstate State Park (Taylors Falls)

■ Wild River State Park (North Brach, Minn.)

■ Governor Knowles State Forest (Grantsburg, Wis.)

■ Chengwatana State Forest (Beroun, Minn.)

■ St. Croix State Park (Hinckley, Minn.)

■ St. Croix State Forest (Sandstone, Minn.)

■ Gordon Dam County Park (Gordon)

■ Brule River State Forest (Solon Springs, Wis.)

■ Chequamegon National Forest (Cable, Wis.)

Kid-Friendly Activities

Outdoors activities for kids can be found aplenty throughout the scenic riverway. By participating, you'll find your children not only come away with great memories but also learn something about nature.

The National Park Service offers the Junior Ranger program, which includes the reward of a St. Croix National Scenic Riverway Junior Ranger patch. To receive a patch, kids must complete a 10-page booklet, available at either visitor center or online, and then successfully demonstrate to a ranger how to put on a life preserver. After a swearing-in ceremony, children receive a certifyicate and pin along with the patch.

State parks in both Minnesota and Wisconsin also offer a variety of programs for children.

Minnesota programs include:

■ **Junior Park Naturalist patches/certificates** – Download from online a nature activity booklet about pinelands, prairies or hardwoods; when children complete them, they can attend a program at the park and receive a free patch and certificate.

■ **Park Explorer patches** – Kids who've completed the Junior Park naturalist program can purchase activity books about nature, history and the earth at the park gift store. Completing the activity book earns the child a Park Explorer patch.

■ **Project Learning Tree** – A number of nature-oriented family games and puzzles are available online via the Minnesota DNR. Volunteers and park rangers sometimes offer nature programs at park visitor centers as well.

Wisconsin state parks offer:

■ **Wisconsin Wildcards** – Kids can collect pocket-sized cards that tell about native species, dangerous plants, and unique spots.

■ **Wisconsin Explorer patches** – Booklets can be downloaded from online that children complete when they visit a park or hike a trail. They then can receive patches for completing the book.

■ **Special programs** – Rangers and volunteers at many parks often offer programs ranging from meeting animals to stargazing at night, from campfire stories to scavenger hunts.

Be sure to check out each state's park system online for a full list of activities on the dates you're visiting.

How to Get There

From the Minneapolis-St. Paul metro area, the riverway can be quickly accessed by heading south on U.S. Hwy. 10 or east on Interstate 94 to the Wisconsin border, or by taking Interstate 35 north and then heading east on roads leading to the riverway, particularly U.S. Hwy. 8 or Minn. Hwys. 70 and 48. Major state and federal highways parallel both the St. Croix and the Namekagon rivers.

From northern Minnesota, take Interstate 35 south to reach the St. Croix. Enter Wisconsin and take U.S. Hwy 53 to reach the Namekagon.

From Iowa, take Interstate 35 north. Use the same crossroads as for the Minneapolis-St. Paul metro area.

From Chicago, southern Wisconsin, and northern Illinois, take Interstate 94 north. Wis. Hwy. 35
in Hudson or Minn. Hwy. 95 in Afton provides access to much of the St. Croix while exiting north on
Hwy. 53 in Eau Claire, Wis., offers a quick route to
the Namekagon.

From Michigan's Upper Peninsula and northeast
Wisconsin, take either U.S. Hwy. 2 or U.S. Hwy. 8
west. Both roads intersect with U.S. Hwy. 63 for ac-
cessing the Namekagon and either Wis. Hwy. 35 or
Interstate 35 for the St. Croix.

Major bridges crossing the St. Croix River, from
south to north, are:

■ U.S. Hwy 10 (Prescott)

■ Interstate 94 (Hudson)

■ Wis. Hwy. 64 (Stillwater; being rebuilt north of
town)

■ Minn. Hwy. 243 (Osceola)

■ U.S. Hwy. 8 (Taylors Falls-St. Croix Falls)

■ Minn./Wis. Hwy. 70 (west of Grantsburg)

■ Minn. Hwy. 48/Wis. Hwy. 77 (east of Hinckley;
west of Danbury)

■ Wis. Hwy. 35 (northeast of Danbury)

Major bridges crossing the Namekagon River,
from west to east, are:

■ Wis. Hwy. 77 (east of Danbury and later north
of Hayward)

■ U.S. Hwy. 53 (Trego)

■ U.S. Hwy. 63 (Trego and later south of Cable)

■ County Road M (east of Cable)

When to Visit

The best months to day hike the scenic riverway are May through September. Depending on the year, April and October also can be pleasant.

As with the rest of the Midwest, summers can be humid, especially July and August. Rain also can occur on afternoons when the morning is sunny, so always check the weather forecast before heading out.

November through March usually is too cold for day hiking. Once snow falls, the trails typically are used by skiers or snowmobilers, though snowshoeing often is an option. Early spring often means muddy trails thanks to snowmelt and rainfall.

Maps

Maps showing hiking trails, campgrounds, parking lots and other facilities are available online at http://hikeswithtykes.com/hittinthetrail_trailmaps. html.

St. Croix River Trails

The majority of day hiking trails along the St. Croix run in the riverway from Prescott north to Danbury, with an additional cluster around Solon Springs. This is where the bulk of the state parks, forests, and natural areas and other public facilities along the riverway are located. The riverway's visitor center is in St. Croix Falls.

Carpenter St. Croix Valley Nature Center

South River Bluff Trail

Day hikers can enjoy a walk down a bluff to the St. Croix River and then through an apple orchard at the Carpenter St. Croix Valley Nature Center in the southeast Twin Cities.

A nonprofit aimed at preserving wildlife habitat and providing educational opportunities about nature, Carpenter St. Croix Valley is free and offers a number of quality programs through the year. The facility is open every day from 8 a.m. to 4:30 p.m. except on Easter, Thanksgiving, Christmas and New Year's Day.

The South River Bluff Trail and a paved trail connecting it to the visitor center runs about 0.95-miles round trip to the shores of the St. Croix. This trail heads through the heart of the center's 425-acre main property in Minnesota; a separate 300-acre restored prairie and wooded bluffs are on a nature preserve in Wisconsin.

To reach the nature center, from U.S. Hwy. 10 take Minn. Hwy. 21 (aka as St. Croix Trail) north and watch for the signs; the center is on the right/east in about two miles.

Once on the center entry road, park in the northern lot.

Check out the interpretive center northeast of the parking lot for several exhibits and displays

about the Lower St. Croix Valley. A paved trail de-
parts from the center's north side.

Follow the trail east, avoiding the turnoffs onto
other trails (Save them for a later visit!). Most of this
area is open, so be sure to don suntan lotion or
wear a sunhat during summer.

The trail soon curves south; at each of the next
three trail junctions, continue heading south. A
wetlands is to the east/left with a tree line in the
distance that turns an array of reds, yellows and
browns each autumn.

Soon the pathway makes a hairpin turn north and
reaches the unpaved South River Bluff Trail. Take
this down the ridge to the river's edge, which is on
the other side of the Railroad Bed Trail. Upon
reaching the river, you're about halfway through
the hike. The far shoreline is Wisconsin.

The St. Croix River there is close to its widest
before flowing into the Mississippi River just a
couple of miles south in Prescott, Wis.

Upon taking in the great views, turn back, returning the way you came. However, if it's autumn,
at the next junction after making the hairpin turn
north go left/west. The trail passes through a small
wooded area, then heads south into the apple orchard.

The orchard was started by the center's name-
sakes, Thomas and Edna Carpenter, in the 1940s.
Thirteen types of apples grow at the center; you'll
be able to purchase most of them in mid-Septem-

ber.

Staying on the orchard's west side, the trail exits into the Apple Shack, which sells apples and honey grown at the center, as well as food ranging from pumpkins and squash to jams and syrups. Decorative corn is sold in autumn.

Leave through the Apple Shack's other side into the southern parking lot. Follow this back to the northern parking lot where your vehicle is.

St. Croix Bluffs Regional Park
St. Croix Bluffs Trail

Hiking families can scramble down a bluff to a St. Croix River beach on a forested trail at St. Croix Bluffs Regional Park north of Hastings, Minn.

Few people other than locals know about the 579-acre county park, which includes prairie, ravines and shoreline. The four miles of trails in the park have no official names, but for convenience sake, I've christened this the St. Croix Bluffs Trail, named for the geographical feature the 1-mile round trip follows.

Autumn marks a perfect time to hike the trail; it's aglow with golds and reds as leaves change their color. Day use permits are required for vehicles to enter the park.

To reach the trail, from U.S. Hwy 10, go north on Minn. Hwy. 21 (aka as St. Croix Trail South). Turn right/east on 102nd Street South then turn right/ south onto 102nd Street Lane South, parking in the first lot on the right.

The trail heads from the lot into the woodline. The path meanders about, generally heading east to the river as roughly paralleling the park road.

In about a quarter mile, you'll reach the first trail junction; go right/southeast. The trail remains in the woodline and continues to parallel the park road.

From there, the trail drops steeply in elevation – about 250 feet – as you descend the bluff to the river. The parking lot was at about 850 feet elevation while the blue river below hits the shoreline at around 698 feet.

About 0.37 miles into the hike, you'll pass through a parking lot, virtually the only unshaded portion of the walk. Then at 0.5 miles the trail reaches the boat landing. Cross it to the beach and cool your dawgs in the St. Croix.

There are picnic tables near the parking lot.

After resting a bit, head back the way you came to your vehicle.

Kinnickinnic State Park
Purple Trail

Day hikers are certain to spot wildlife on the Purple Trail at the southernmost state park along the St. Croix River.

The 1.2-mile loop, which includes a segment of the Yellow Trail, takes hikers along a first-class trout stream at Kinnickinnic State Park. Though a compact park at a little more than 1200 acres, it contains an old-growth oak forest, restored prairies, and a river delta.

To reach the park, from Wis. Hwy. 29 northeast of Prescott, Wis., take County Road F north for about 5.5 miles. Turn left/west onto 820th Avenue then left/south into the park; follow the entry road west all of the way to its end and park in the St. Croix Picnic Area Lot.

An access trail to the main course begins in the lot's western corner. Upon reaching the Purple Trail, turn right/north. Most of the trees in this area of Wisconsin were cut by pioneers and 19th century logging companies, but the trail here passes through one of the few woodlands to escape the ax.

Wildlife abounds as well in this area. Watch for white-tailed deer, raccoons, rabbits and squirrels. Hikers have spotted weasels, gray fox, red fox and even beaver nearby.

In about 600 feet from the access trail, you'll pass a path to the swim area. Continuing on the main trail, the woods soon gives way to a restored prairie.

This region was plowed under by the area's first white settlers but since 1972 (when the state park was established) have been among 50 acres of land at the park restored to original prairie. Watch for partridge, ringneck pheasants and other birds that prefer grasslands.

You'll soon reach a junction with the Yellow Trail; go right/south on it through more prairie. In about 600 feet, you'll cross the park entry road, so make sure any little ones with you watch for traffic.

The Yellow Trail then rejoins the Purple Trail; go right/south onto the latter. After a junction with the Orange Trail, the Kinnickinnic River should come in view to the left/south. You're on a bluff overlooking the river; don't get too close to the edge, though, as the limestone cliff is a straight drop down.

White pines line the river, which is popular with anglers for its brown trout. Watch for mink slinking along the banks looking for food.

Rounding the picnic area, head into the overlook on the left/west to see the Kinnickinnic River Delta with the St. Croix River. Sediment from the Kinnickinnic reduces the St. Croix's width here by about 75 percent.

The result is a faster current, which during winter leaves the St. Croix ice-free. Because of that, bald eagles enjoy a year-round fishing area, so keep your eyes to the sky for the bird of prey.

The access trail to the parking lot is directly across from the overlook.

If time and energy allows, consider extending the hike by adding the rest of the Yellow Trail; to do that, at the first junction of the Purple/Yellow trails, go left/north onto the latter. The 1.2-mile Yellow Trail (You'll only do about a mile of it for a

1.8-mile hike total.) loops along the forest and prairie edge. A flat trail, it offers the opportunity to spot wild turkeys. When the Yellow rejoins the Purple, go left/south onto the latter.

Alternately, enjoy a dip into the St. Croix River at its swim area that the Purple Trail passed at its start. There's a small sand beach at the swim area, and the St. Croix is one of the Midwest's cleanest waterways.

Entrance fees are required to enter the park and vary based on whether or not you're in a vehicle with Wisconsin license plates and the amount of time you wish to spend there. Rates for one hour in a Wisconsin vehicle are the least expensive while annual passes for out-of-state vehicles cost the most.

Other Kinnickinnic State Park Trails

■ **Red Trail** – The 1.6-mile hike heads through prairie alongside a forest's edge. Among the highlights is the Vulture's Peak area. Near the park entrance, the set of two loops can be accessed from the park's first two parking lot.

■ **Blue Trail** – The 0.7-mile out-and-back trail (1.4-miles round trip) gives hikers the opportunity to explore gorges and coulees into the Kinnickinnic River Valley. Access the wooded trail from the second parking area past the park entrance. Add the 0.1-mile (0.2-miles round trip) Brown Trail, which serves as a sledding hill in winter, to extend the hike.

■ **Yellow Trail** – The 1.2-mile loop edges a forest and prairie area. Watch for deer, pheasants and turkeys along the trail. The Kinni Overlook Lot is a good place to start; the trail can be extended by adding the Green, Orange or Purple trails.

■ **Orange Trail** – A wooded out-and-back trail atop the Kinnickinnic River bluffs, it runs for 0.5 miles (1-mile round trip). Park at the Kinni Overlook Lot and access it via the Yellow Trail; add the Purple and Yellow trails for a longer walk.

■ **Green Trail** – The trail loops about the outside of a prairie area under restoration and is an excellent place to spot partridge, pheasants and other birds. Access it via the Yellow Trail; from the Kinni Overlook Lot, go left/north on the Yellow for a 1.6-mile round trip (The Green Trail itself is 1.1-miles long).

Afton State Park
North River Trail

Day hikers can enjoy a pleasant walk alongside the widest section of the St. Croix River on the North River Trail at Minnesota's Afton State Park.

The 2.2-miles round trip also offers the opportunity for a swim to cool off when the walk is all over.

To reach the park, take Minn. Hwy. 21 about 4.5 miles south of Afton, Minn. Turn east into the park at the Minn. Hwy. 20 intersection. Follow the entry road to a set of seven parking lots in front of the visitor center; any one of them will work with a trailhead or a connecting trail on each lot's east side; just always be sure to veer left/north when coming to the first trail junction. If taking the south-ernmost parking lot along the entry road, you'll add about 0.3 miles one-way to the hike.

The trail gradually veers toward the St. Croix, which at this point on its course is known as Lake St. Croix because of its width. Lake St. Croix stretches south from Stillwater, Minn., to Prescott, Wis., where the river joins the Mississippi.

The river reaches its widest at 1.25 miles just north of the state park. Its deepest point is 78 feet.

Between the parking lot and river, the North River Trail passes picnic areas, a shelter, and tele-scopes for viewing the scenic Wisconsin side across the sapphire-colored water. The trail heads by the swimming beach about a half-mile to 0.75 miles into the hike.

As the trail stays close to the river below the bluff, trees along the way can be underwater dur-ing spring flooding and other high water years.

Once away from the beach, the trail becomes a tranquil, unpaved path. Your only company likely will be the birds of prey circling for fish and the number of recreational boats enjoying the river.

This section of the river is extremely popular among anglers. More than 60 fish species call Lake St. Croix home; among them are walleye and muskies (Minnesota's and Wisconsin's state fish respectively), northern pike, largemouth and small-mouth bass, bluegill, and crappie. White bass is particularly abundant near the park.

Some fish size is exceptional. Minnesota's state record catfish – coming in at 70 pounds – was caught in Lake St. Croix. Fishermen also have hauled in lake sturgeon weighing more than 50 pounds. Some channel catfish weigh in excess of 25 pounds.

At 1.1-1.4 miles from the visitor center, the trail veers west away from the river and climbs the hill up the bluff. This marks a good time to turn back. Before returning to your vehicle, stop at the visitor center to learn more about the river and ecosystems at the park.

This also is a bicycle trail, so be aware of the two-wheelers. During spring and early summer, always don repellant for mosquitoes (Minnesota's unofficial state bird).

Other Afton State Park Trails

■ **Deer Valley Loop** – For a solid workout and great vistas, try this 2.2-mile trail, which heads up and down the bluff overlooking the St. Croix. You'll need to first hike 1.3 miles of connecting trails to reach the trailhead for a 4.8-mile round trip.

■ **Prairie Loop** – The 2.1-mile trail circles a blufftop prairie and can be extended by taking loops off the main route. A mile of connecting trails are needed to reach the trailhead for a 4.1-mile round trip.

■ **South River Trail** – The 3.2-mile round-trip trail rambles alongside the St. Croix River through a woods. It offers great views of the scenic Wisconsin shoreline.

■ **Trout Brook Loop** – The trail heads alongside and over Trout Brook, a St. Croix tributary, then behind a small border that borders the stream. Though only 1.5-miles long, you'll need to hike 2.3 miles of connecting trails to its trailhead, resulting in a 6.1-mile round trip.

Willow River State Park
Hidden Ponds Nature (Black) Trail

Families can enjoy a fun day of discovering nature with a hike on the Hidden Ponds Nature Trail at Willow River State Park in Hudson, Wis.

The half-mile interpretive loop is paved, level and out of the wind, ideal for young children. Also known as the Black Trail (because of its color on park maps), the walking path is right next to the park's nature center and a short stroll to the park's swimming beach.

Though the park technically is not in the scenic riverway, Willow River flows into the St. Croix. At 61.1 miles long, the Willow is one of the St. Croix's most important – and beautiful – tributaries.

To reach the trail, from Interstate 94's Exit 4 take County Road U north. In about two miles, County

Road U ends at County Road A; go right/northeast at this junction. The park entrance road is another two miles on the left/west. Follow the park road to the nature center parking lot. It's about a half-hour drive from downtown St. Paul, Minn.

The trailhead is next to the nature center at the parking lot's southeast corner. A small stem takes you to the main loop.

Be sure to pick up a guide at the trailhead. Numbered posts run all along the trail, providing great opportunities to teach children to learn about the oak forest and wetlands they're passing through.

If quiet, you'll probably spot white-tailed deer along the trail, especially at dusk. Songbirds also are plentiful. In mid-September, blackberries can be found along the trailside.

After completing the loop, stop in the nature center. Various displays and exhibits focus on west-central Wisconsin's natural and cultural history. A wildflower garden just outside the center offers 20 common species – such as black-eyed Susan, blazing star, and New England aster – and some of them almost always are in bloom from spring through autumn.

If heading to the park during summer, check online to see what programs are planned at the nature center. The center is open year around. Also, be forewarned: the nature center has a gift shop.

After the nature center, make a full day of it with

a walk over to the Little Falls Lake swimming beach, just a few dozen feet northeast of the parking lot. Be sure to pack bathing suits, towels, and sand toys.

A final note: Leashed pets are not allowed on the Hidden Ponds Nature Trail, though they may be taken on other park trails. The park is open every day of the year from 6 a.m. to 11 p.m.

Burkhardt (Pink) Trail

A walk alongside a scenic river gorge, a waterfall, and some impressive overlooks await hikers on the park's Burkhardt Trail.

The trail actually is three miles of connecting paths. It's also known as the Pink Trail because of its color on state park maps.

To reach this trail, pass the park's entrance on County Road A and then turn left onto County Road I. Take a left onto River Road (aka 115th Avenue) and then make a quick left into the River Road parking lot (You'll need to pay an entrance fee or sport an annual state park pass.). The trailhead is on the parking lot's south side.

The path begins by heading southwest along the Willow River bottoms. The marsh-like region boasts tall grasses and during summer a number of wildflowers. Watch for white-tailed deer in the brush, eagles soaring overhead, and during summer butterflies and dragonflies flitting about. Frogs and a variety of birds also are abundant along the riverfront.

Upon coming to the first fork, go left into a wooded area and then into a large meadow. Aspen, oak, maple and of course willow trees abound. At the next fork, again go left. You'll head onto a bluff to an impressive overlook of the waterway and the gorge it has cut.

The trail then heads downward. At the next fork, veer left for the multi-level Willow River Falls. The rock on the gorge walls' lowest levels is about 600 million years old.

You can take a stairwell about 100-feet down to the falls. Sometimes you'll catch people wading through the falls; this is not advised for small children.

You can treat the trail to the falls as a spur and simply head back the way you came, or you can continue onward. If choosing the latter, cross the wood footbridge over the river but then turn back or you'll find yourself on another trail on the wrong side of the waterway.

Upon turning back, the trail meanders northward, ultimately forming a loop.

At the next trail intersection, go left. You'll then be heading back to the parking lot. At the next fork, turn left again, and you'll find yourself on the trail winding along the river bottoms, which is where you started.

Depending on whether or not you turned around at the falls, the hike ranges from two to four miles in length.

Other Willow River State Park Trails

■ **Knapweed (Orange) Trail** – The trail runs for 0.9 miles one-way alongside an effort to restore prairie as it existed in Wisconsin before pioneers arrived during the 1800s. Among the plants you may notice – especially in late June to early July when it blossoms – is the purple knapweed, the trail's namesake but unfortunately an invasive species that actually threatens the prairie and other ecosystems.

■ **Little Falls (Green) Trail** – The 0.7-mile paved trail rambles alongside Little Falls Lake between Little Falls Dam and the campground. A variety of waterfowl can be spotted from it.

■ **Mound (White) Trail** – Located in an often overlooked section of the state park, the 1.1-mile Mound Trail offers views of the Willow River and a glacial mound (a hill that resisted erosion during the last ice age) on the opposite shore.

■ **Nelson Farm (Silver) Trail** – The state park's newest trail opened in summer 2012. The 3.7-mile trail heads from a bridge on the Trout Brook (Purple) Trail through several ecosystems to the lake's north side.

■ **Oak Ridge (Brown) Trail** – Hikers can learn about geological features created during the last ice age on this 1.1-mile trail. It heads from the beach through hardwood forests.

■ **Pioneer (Yellow) Trail** – Among the best views of Willow Falls can be seen from an overlook on the 1.2-mile trail. It also passes the gravesites of the area's first white settlers.

■ **Trout Brook (Purple) Trail** – This 1.4-mile loop takes hikers through red pine stands and open prairie. You'll be able to spot great blue heron, ducks and snapping turtles along the way.

Stillwater Area Trails
Brown's Creek Park and Nature Preserve Ski Trail segment

Most people go to Stillwater, Minn., for its trendy shops and great restaurants in an historical urban setting. And while there's not much in town for backpackers, there are some good day hikes for families before they stop downtown for a classy meal.

The Brown's Creek Park and Nature Preserve Ski Trail offers the best day hiking option in the Stillwater area. Close to the scenic riverway, it gives you a good sense of what a blufftop woodlands area is like.

Located in the Brown's Creek Park and Nature Preserve, the trail actually is a number of short connecting paths constructed for cross country skiing and is run by the City of Stillwater and the Stillwater Cross Country Ski Association. It remains open when snow is not on the ground, however; a

0.9-mile segment that forms a loop is described here.

To reach the trail, from Minn. Hwy. 36, go north on County Road 15/Manning Avenue, then turn right/east onto County Road 64/McKusick Road North. Past Maryland Avenue North, beyond where the railroad tracks veer away from the road, is a parking lot on the right. From the lot's southwest corner, walk the stem trail into the woods.

Take the second junction for a trail going left. Pass through the next junction. The trail here is largely shaded by a mix of deciduous and evergreen trees and crosses Brown's Creek, for which the park and nature preserve is named.

Brown's Creek marks one of the few waterways in the Minneapolis-St. Paul metro area that sports a fishable trout population. It runs for nearly 10 miles, starting a good five miles north of Stillwater before flowing into the St. Croix just north of town. Since 1955, the state has stocked the creek with brown trout.

Soon the trail runs easterly along the south side of a wetlands formed by Brown's Creek. Upon reaching the first trail junction that allows you to go left/northwest, take it. You'll double back across a wet area, so late summer and autumn, and usually a few days after a rain, mark the best time to hike the nature area.

As the trail veers north, it borders Brown's Creek and a wooded area before reaching the stem trail leading to the parking lot.

St. Croix Boom Site Trail

Families can day hike a historical remnant from the St. Croix River's lumber baron days just north of Stillwater.

The St. Croix Boom Site Trail runs a mere 0.4-miles round trip but makes for a scenic afternoon diversion. A century-and-a-half-ago ago, the site was a bustling center of activity where men pulled logs from the St. Croix River and sent them on their way to nearby sawmills.

To reach the trail, from downtown Stillwater drive north on Minn. Hwy. 95. Watch for the signs; after Pawnee Avenue North, there's a turnoff for the Boom Site on the right/east. Park in the spaces along the looping access road. The trailhead is south of the lot's access road with the Boom Site a mere 50-foot walk down a staircase to the beach.

Throughout the mid- and late-1800s, lumber-jacks downed whole forests across northern Minnesota and Wisconsin, branded each log with the sawmill it was to go to, and floated the timber down the St. Croix River to its destination.

When the St. Croix Boom Company went bust upstream near Marine on St. Croix, several Stillwater lumber barons bought the business and moved it north of town. The boom company drew the timber from the river then sorted and delivered it to the correct sawmill in Stillwater. All through the 1870s, logs would back up some 15 miles on the river during midsummer as awaiting for the boom company to pull them out.

By the early 20th century, most Northwoods forests were gone, and the boom site ceased operation in 1914. As the economy changed and generations passed, the sorting center was largely forgotten.

The National Park Service discovered it during a 1975 survey while identifying historical sites along the St. Croix. Today, it's a National Historic Landmark.

At the bottom of the stairs, hikers can head up and down the pleasant beach below a sandstone bluff. The beach peters out about 600 feet downstream and heads roughly 400 feet upstream to a nice point overlooking a river island.

William O'Brien State Park
Riverside Trail

Day hikers can learn about the power of floods on the St. Croix River via the Riverside Trail at William O'Brien State Park in Minnesota.

The 1.5-mile trail loops through a floodplain and typically is open during summer and autumn when water levels have gone down. Don't think of this area as a swamp, though – you'll find rest areas (some with benches) about every 900 feet on the trail, as well as interpretive signs.

To reach the trail, from Marine on St. Croix, Minn., take Minn. Hwy. 95 north into the park. Turn right/east onto O'Brien Trail North/County Road 33. The road curves south, dead ending in a parking area alongside Lake Alice. The trail begins at the picnic grounds immediately east of the parking lot.

At the amphitheater, the trail curves east then north again as paralleling a back channel of the St. Croix River. The fresh scent of pine needles upon the trail and the gentle rush of water along the river's rock walls instantly lulls you into a feeling of serenity.

About 0.3 miles from the amphitheater, shortly after passing a stem trail leading to a campground, the back channel joins the main channel. Roughly half of the trail follows the river, mainly through a good mix of hardwoods common to a floodplain forest in this region. During autumn, their leaves turn gold, red, orange and brown. Across the water is Wisconsin, and with the two undeveloped shorelines, tranquility reigns.

A little more than halfway through the hike, the trail veers from the river and follows a small stream that flows from the bluffs into the St. Croix. Frogs make their home along the creek in large numbers, and you're likely to hear them through the day.

The trail then curves south and soon crosses O'Brien Trail North. This marks the steepest section of the trail as it rises and drops about 40 feet over a knoll. Next the trail squeezes between the road and Lake Alice. The lake was named for Alice O'Brien, whose donation of 180 acres in honor of her father, William, launched the park.

Springs at Lake Alice's north end feeds it through the year, ensuring the water remains clean and blue all summer. Keep an eye to the sky for eagles and hawks looking for a meal in the lake. Geese and ducks usually can be spotted floating about, so if you have little ones, bring some dried bread they can toss into the water to feed the waterfowl.

The Riverside Trail is wheelchair accessible. It also has restrooms and a swimming area on Lake Alice at trail's end, so be sure to pack your kids' swimming trunks.

Other William O'Brien State Park Trails

The rest of the park's trails can be divided into two clusters, with three specific parking lots offering access to several trailheads.

Wedge Savanna Trail Cluster

Take Minn. Hwy. 95 to the park entrance. At the first junction, go left/southeast then turn at the next left/southwest into a parking lot. Trails that can be easily reached from this lot include:

■ **Wedge Hill Savanna Trail (small loop)** – This 0.5-mile loop sits on a prairie atop the river bluff. From the parking lot, take the connecting trail left/west to the Savanna Trail trailhead, going left at the first junction.

■ **Wetland Trail** – The 2.2-mile loop heads around a blufftop wetlands; with connector trails, the hike runs about 2.6-miles round trip. At the trailhead for the Wedge Hill Savanna Trail, go right/north for 0.1 miles to the Wetland Trail loop.

■ **Beaver Lodge Trail** – The 0.7-mile loop encircles a wetlands where beavers have created a small pond; you'll hike 1.7 miles round trip with the connecting trails. Upon reaching the Wedge Hill Savanna Trail, stay on that loop's western side. At the next junction at the bottom of the loop, go left/west 0.2 miles, passing a junction for the Savanna Trail's larger loop; after that, go left/south onto Beaver Lodge Trail loop.

■ **Hardwood Hills Trail** – Though this 1.1-mile loop trail through a forested area at the park's northern boundary heads off another cluster's trail, the Savanna Trail parking lot is the shortest route to it; you'll walk 4.1-miles round trip with the connecting trails. At the Wedge Hill Savanna Trail junction, go right/north, then at the Wetland Trail junction, head right/north; after passing below the railroad overpass, go right/northwest onto the Woodland Edge Trail. The next junction is the Hardwood Hills Trail. Ferns abound on the trail as well as the ovenbirds unique song.

Prairie Overlook Cluster

From Broadway Street in Marine on St. Croix,

Minn., take County Road 4/Ostrum Trail north into the park. After going under the railroad overpass, turn right/north into a parking lot. Trails accessible from this lot include:

■ **Prairie Overlook Trail** – The 1.6-mile narrow loop with a pond at its center heads through both open country and a woods. From the parking lot, take the 0.1-mile stem trail to the loop.

■ **Woodland Edge Trail** – This 2.1-mile loop runs through a forest; you'll hike 3.6 miles total with the connecting trails. From the parking lot, take the stem trail to the Prairie Overlook Trail and head up its west side; at the first junction, go either left or right onto the Woodland Edge Trail loop. You can add 1.1 miles to the loop by taking the adjoining Hardwood Hills Trail.

■ **Rolling Hills Savanna Trail** – This 1.1-mile loop gently rolls through a small woods; connecting trails make for a 4.1-mile round trip. Head up the Prairie Overlook Trail's west side. At the first junction, go left onto the Woodland Edge Trail and then take the next left/south onto the Rolling Hills Trail.

Osceola Area Trails
Cascade Falls Trail

A 25-foot waterfall awaits hikers on a very short trail in the village of Osceola, Wis.

The Cascade Falls Trail runs less than a couple

of hundred feet – and most of that is up and down a stairs from the street to the glen where the falls sits.

To reach the trailhead, take Wis. Hwy. 35 into Osceola. As entering downtown, the highway becomes North Cascade Street. Park anywhere downtown along the street.

Signs mark the trailhead, located on the street's east side across from First Avenue. To reach the trail, a steep staircase that looks like it was extracted from a fire tower heads from the sidewalk to Willkie Glen.

Majestic trees shade the staircase and glen in green. You'll be able to hear the waterfall's roar from the sidewalk – and easily spot it once you reach the glen.

Osceola Creek drops over the natural falls as it flows westward on its way to the St. Croix River. Between the village and the river, the creek descends 100 feet in altitude, but this waterfalls is the only large drop.

The falls wouldn't exist if not for the river. At the end of the last ice age some 10,000 years ago, floodwaters from melting glaciers carved out a large gorge. The waterfall is a one of the vertical wall cuts in that gorge. It measures 30 feet across.

The village itself might not exist if not for the falls. Osceola was settled because the falls could support industry; in the late 1800s, it powered a mill.

The smaller and narrower Geiger Falls is upstream on Osceola Creek, but there's no hiking path between it and Cascade Falls.

The best time to hike the trail is in spring when snow melt increases the amount of water flowing over the falls. Another good time to visit: at night when the village lights up the falls using LED lighting to mimic the glow of the full moon upon the water; coloring is changed for the seasons.

A dirt footpath does lead from Cascade Falls to the St. Croix. The village has plans to improve the walkway into a more accessible trail.

In the centuries ahead, the waterfalls actually will be its own undoing – the splash of water at its base has created a kickpoint in the vertical wall that is slowly eroding and undercutting the drop, which one day will cause it to collapse. The waterfalls then will become a cascades, or series of rock steps, that the creek flows over.

Ridge View (Osceola and Chisago) Trails

Fantastic river views beneath a lush forest canopy await hikers on the Ridge View Trails near Osceola.

Not to be confused with Ridgeview Trail at the adjacent Osceola Bedrock Glades State Natural Area, this pair of trails actually is two loops that only locals really know about. They run through the scenic riverway and the Osceola State Fish Hatchery on a bluff overlooking a St. Croix River back channel.

To reach the two loops, take Wis. Hwy. 35 north of Osceola and turn north onto County Road S. The two trailheads are on the road's west (or driver's) side. Both trailheads have their own parking areas off of the road. Just beyond 93rd Avenue is the southernmost parking area, which actually is an excellent trailhead for either loop.

From that trailhead, head west. At the first fork, continue straight to hike the Chisago Loop. Slightly more than a mile long, it's the northern trail.

Alternatively, at the fork you can head left/south, for the Osceola Loop, which is about twice as long as its counterpart. Either trail ranges from easy to moderate in difficulty, so the distance you can handle, especially if you have children along, really determines which one to take.

If heading onto the Chisago Loop, you'll hike clockwise around the trail. It's mostly level and sometimes covered in a bed of pine needles or ancient, billion-year-old trap rock. You'll see a number of these basalt outcroppings along the way. Some neat spurs off the trail offer great views of the river below.

About two-thirds of the way around, be careful of taking a fork to the right/north, lest you end up at the second of the road's two parking lots (which is the one where you didn't park your vehicle).

If opting for the Osceola Loop, upon reaching the main trail, go left/south, so you take it clockwise. This saves the best views for the last half of the hike.

You'll begin by heading through a pine and deciduous forest in which the canopy arches over the trail. About halfway through as you turn north, between the trees you can see river's back channel and hear the rush of a rapids-filled stream in the canyon below the bluffs. Watch for pits off of the trail; they are believed to have been made many decades ago by Native Americans.

Either trail is excellent for viewing birds – scarlet tanagers, eagles, turkeys, grouse – and other forest-loving wildlife. Woodland plants you're likely to spot include marsh marigolds and large maple trees.

Osceola Bedrock Glades State Natural Area
Ridgeview Trail

Travelers to Wisconsin can hike across billion-year-old lava flows while seeing a rare, unique glade ecosystem when taking the Ridgeview Trail at the Osceola Bedrock Glades State Natural Area.

Located north of Osceola, from Wis. Hwy. 35 turn north on County Road S. After passing 93rd Avenue and crossing two creeks (a total of 1.1 miles), turn left (or west) onto the next unpaved road and park there. The trailhead is to the southeast along the roadside.

The trail leads south into the natural area. You

can take two loops, one short (0.9-mile loop) and the other long (1.5-mile loop; if taking the uphill route, 2.1-mile loop). You may have to briefly walk cross-country on a deer trail, but the vegetation generally is low and easy to pass.

Begin by heading a tenth of a mile roughly southwest toward a hill. The greenery of the thin-trunked trees forms a marked contrast with the black rock jutting out of the hard ground. For 200 million years, lava flowed across the region, which at the time was a rift zone where the land to the west and that to the east shifted apart from one another.

At the hill's base, turn right and walk about a third of a mile. Because of the hard, flat volcanic bedrock beneath your feet, very few plants can grow here. Most common are ferns, mosses, low-growing herbs and fungi.

The area itself is rare. In fact, only three other bedrock glade ecosystems exist in Wisconsin.

To take the short trail, upon reaching the hill's corner head up to its top for 0.3 miles. The hill summit is about half of this distance. The summit's basalt outcroppings feels more like a West Coast mountain top than a Midwestern hill. At the hill's base, upon coming to County Road S, go north 0.2 miles back to your vehicle.

For the longer trail, instead of turning at the hill's corner go 0.1 miles northwest to a rock outcropping. The black, moss-covered rocks gives the

area an otherworldly feel. Walk around it, and enjoy your blufftop view overlooking the St. Croix
River; you're at about 876 feet elevation. If children
are with you, make sure they stay back from the
bluff's edge.

The trail passes through oak woodland and in
areas where the volcanic rock is close to the surface, the bedrock glade. The rare prairie flame
flower can be spotted here. In September, the
white arrow-leaved aster blooms, which makes for
an interesting accent color before tree leaves have
changed to their fall colors.

Despite the harsh environment for plants, a
number of animals live in the bedrock glade. With
the thin trees, owls are easy to spot. Around Labor
Day, some interesting insects come out. The giant
swallowtail caterpillar, which looks more like a
knotty branch than a furry little creature, can be
seen crawling on prickly ash, and you'll likely sight
a lyre-tipped spreadwing perching on a twig-like
branch. During the summer, mosquitoes can be
ubiquitous, so don't forget the bug repellent.

The trail loops 0.7 miles around the back of the
hill. At about 0.2 miles on this loop, you will join a
jeep trail, which you can follow for more ease of
walking.

On the southeast side of hill's base, when the
trail reaches County Road S, head north for a little
more than 0.2 miles back to your vehicle.

Alternately, you can follow a trail west up to the

hill summit and then upon coming down it on its west side, rejoin the trail where you began your loop, retracing it back to your vehicle.

Wisconsin Interstate State Park
Summit Rock Trail

On the scenic Summit Rock Trail, families can hike across or see the results of the three most significant geological events to shape the riverway.

The trail takes hikers to the highest point at Interstate State Park in St. Croix Falls, Wis. It runs atop billion-year-old lava flows, the sands of a 500-million-year-old sea, and at the edge of a massive glacial flood from 10,000 years ago.

Interstate State Park sits off Wis. Hwy. 35 just a half-mile mile south of U.S. Hwy. 8 along the St. Croix River. A national park pass will get you in for free.

Follow Park Road into Interstate. As it heads south and reaches Lake O' the Dalles, look for the parking lot on the road's right side. The trailhead is at the lot's north end.

Expect the park to be busy. It boasts visitor numbers on par with national parks. Additional parking lots can be found on the road's left side.

The trail heads to the bluff's highest point and is a dirt surface, so expect an uneven and steep walk at times. Small sections of the 0.5-mile trail (one-way) consist of stone and wooden steps through a forested area.

Moss and autumn leaves cover the surrounding rock and ground. Maples, basswood and eastern white pines line the trail. At the top, prickly pear cactus even can be spotted amid the outcroppings.

Though the park includes a campground and is near an urban area, wildlife abounds. Don't be surprised to see squirrel, raccoon, deer and dozens of bird varieties along the way. Fox, muskrat and beaver live closer to the river.

The bluff wouldn't exist if not for a major geological event dating some 1.1 billion years ago. At that time, massive lava flows covered this region of the world. As you near the trail's top, the black basalt rock you pass and step upon dates from that era.

The highlight of the hike without question is the incredible view of the riverway from the summit. Looking north, the Old Man of the Dalles rock formation is visible just beyond glacial potholes.

The rocks making up the Old Man actually were laid some 515 million years ago when this region sat under a warm shallow sea near the equator. As sediments piled up and were covered over the eons, they hardened into rock; the landscape finally rose above the sea about 345 million years ago.

Then about 10,000 years ago at the end of the last ice age, a glacial torrent swept through the area. This flood carved the intriguing cliff formation.

During the flood, giant eddies from the flow

drilled holes into the landscape; these are the potholes between the summit and the Dalles. The largest glacial potholes in the world are just across the river in Minnesota.

Return to the parking lot the same way you came for a 1-mile round trip. If you have a full day to spend, a plethora of other activities are held at the park; check at the visitor center for a schedule.

Lake O' the Dalles Trail

Families can hike around and even swim in a lake that once was part of the St. Croix River at Wisconsin Interstate State Park.

The Lake O' the Dalles Trail circles its namesake, a 23-acre lake, in a 1-mile loop. Nicely lined with hardwood trees, the lakeside trail is relatively flat with a few stairs.

Park in the same lot as for the Summit Rock Trail. The trailhead is on the lot's north side; head left/west onto the trail, passing the picnic area.

During the past 10,000 years, the St. Croix River has changed its course several times. The small ravines across the park indicate where it once ran. During those course changes, the river hollowed out this backwater lake with sediment then filling in the space between it and the St. Croix's current course. No more than 12 feet deep, the Lake O' the Dalles' bottom is about 99 percent rock.

After the trail circles the lake's north side, it comes to a junction with Echo Canyon Trail. Continue paralleling the lake.

Despite being cut off from the main channel, the picturesque lake recently has been invaded by the non-native curly-leaf pondweed. Originally from Eurasia, the plant lives from the shoreline to depths of up to 15 feet in lakes, where it can displace native plants. It's a problem across the Great Lakes states.

The next two trail junctions are for the River Bluff Trail. The Lake O' the Dalles Trail can be extended by hiking the River Bluff Trail, a 0.7-mile loop that takes hikers between the St. Croix River gorge and the Lake O' the Dalles. The rocks and sparse vegetation gives it a Rocky Mountain feel. If adding that loop, the hike's total length is about 1.6 miles.

The next highlight along the lake trail is a railed fishing pier that you can walk out onto. You'll often find anglers here catching largemouth bass, northern pike, panfish and walleye from the lake.

As following the trail around the lake's west side, the River Bottoms Picnic Area is to the west next to the St. Croix River. Along this side of the lake, about 40 yards of the trail follows the park road.

A footbridge then crosses Dalles Creek as the trail loops back around the lake's south side.

An excellent trail for spotting wildlife, you stand a good chance of seeing white-tailed deer or fox near the lake. Eagles and osprey also are likely as they circle overhead looking for a meal. More rarely, black bear have been spotted plodding about nearby.

The trail then heads up the lake's eastern side to the stone Beach House. The CCC and WPA constructed the rustic building during the Great Depression. A swimming beach is located here. The beach house is near the trailhead, with your parking lot in clear view.

Other Wisconsin Interstate State Park Trails

■ **Eagle Peak Trail** – The trail takes you to the park's highest point, Eagle Peak. Though short at 0.8 miles, the trail climbs 120 feet in elevation, including up stone stairs. The trailhead begins at the Pines Group Camp. A short side trail passes a traprock quarry built by the CCC during the 1930s on its way to South Campground.

■ **Horizon Rock Trail** – The westernmost steps of the Ice Age National Scenic Trail end with this 0.5-mile trail, which runs northwest between the Ice Age Visitor Center and Pothole Trail. From the center, you'll pass a decades-old stone shelter, known as Historic Rock, offering a panoramic view of the river gorge below.

■ **Pothole Trail** – When a flood from melting glaciers swept through at the end of the last ice age, swirling water literally drilled holes into the basalt rock underlying this region. The 0.4-mile loop takes you past a number of these interesting geological features in the park.

■ **Silverbrook Trail** – To get away from the park crowds, hike this 1.2-mile (2.4-miles round trip) trail to the remote, forested southern end. The trail in part follows the original road that connected the village of Osceola to the south with St. Croix Falls to the north. It passes an abandoned copper mine and the Silverbrook Mansion grounds, then reaches the trail's highlight: 18-foot Silverbrook Falls.

■ **Skyline Trail** – The trail runs for 1.6 miles (3.2 miles round trip) southwest from the center to the Pines Group Camp. It first passes the Skyline Nature Trail and then the Ravine Trail. From there, the trail ascends rock-covered ravines to the valley's forested rim.

Minnesota Interstate State Park
Shadow and Angle Rocks Lookout Trails

The northern section of Minnesota Interstate State Park – also known as the Pothole Area – offers day hikers a number of trails for exploring the area's geology and enjoying its scenic beauty.

A pair of interconnecting short trails known as the Shadow and Angle Rocks Lookout Trails begin at the parking lot's southern end; at the drinking fountain go left toward the river.

The path to Shadow Rock Lookout follows the route to the Lower Boat Tour Landing. A side trail leads to a glacial pothole called the Cauldron. The potholes were formed about 10,000 years ago when swirling glacial meltwater sweeping down the river drilled holes into the ancient basalt bedrock.

Back on the main trail, you'll pass through The Squeeze, an exceedingly tight, L-shaped break between two ultra-large chunks of basalt (Warning: Young children may be frightened in the dark, narrow quarters). From there, climb to the Shadow Rock Lookout, which offers a great vista of the St. Croix River and gorge rock formations on the Wisconsin side.

Taking the path that veers away from the Lower Boat Tour Landing leads to the Angle Rock Lookout. You'll first pass a few potholes on your right. At the Lily Pond Pothole, turn right where you'll pass more potholes, including the famous Bottomless Pit and Bake Oven. The trail then briefly joins the Shadow Rock path; go left then at the next junction take a right. When the trail reaches the intersection after that, go right and climb to the top of Angle Rock.

Technically, these paths are part of the Lost Pothole Trail. For a shorter version of that trail, pick up its trailhead on the parking lot's west side. At the first junction, go right so that you take the trail counterclockwise. You'll pass a few baby potholes.

Upon reaching the River Trail junction, go left to the interpretive kiosk then to the drinking fountain. At the parking lot, veer right to the visitor center.

To extend the trail, follow the loop around the visitor center, and for even more walking, add the loop stacked to the north of it.

Other Minnesota Interstate State Park Trails

■ **Picnic Area Loop** – Located in the Milltown Road parking lots, the short trail is handicapped accessible. It makes a square that takes users past the boat ramp and briefly alongside the St. Croix River.

■ **Railroad Trail** – The 1.5-mile Railroad Trail parallels U.S. Hwy. 8 into downtown Taylors Falls, where it passes a historic train depot, and ends at the park's Pothole Area. It can be reached via the Sandstone Bluff Trail (see below); combining the Sandstone and Railroad trails would be a four-mile hike from the Milltown Road parking lots.

■ **River Trail** – Also located in the Milltown Road section, the trail runs 1.25 miles along the river. The route first passes a campground (a connector trail links the campsites to the trail) and then hugs the shoreline where Folsom Island sits in the river. Three overlooks are on the trail, which ends at the park's northern side.

■ **Sandstone Bluff Trail** – The trail heads northwest under Hwy. 8 to a nice vista of the valley and river gorge below. A 1-mile lollipop trail, it's spectacular in autumn with a mix of colors from the orange maples, red sumac, and brilliant yellow oaks.

St. Croix Falls Area Trails
Indianhead Flowage Trail

You can walk atop billion-year-old volcanic rock surrounded by the deep blue of a river and the lush green of a forest on the Indianhead Flowage Trail in the scenic riverway.

Located along Wis. Hwy. 87 about a mile north of St. Croix Falls, Wis., the 1.5-mile trail begins at Lion's Club Park. The trailhead is on the park road's southwest side.

That the path is among the opening miles of Wisconsin's famed Ice Age National Scenic Trail is appropriate. When the last glacier covering this region melted thousands of years ago, massive floods smashed through the area, carving the St. Croix River Valley out of volcanic basalt bedrock that formed some 750 million years before dinosaurs walked the Earth.

The trail winds through forests and wetlands with bridges crossing streams flowing into the St. Croix River. At some spots, the trail comes within 20 feet of that waterway.

A warm, dry spring day marks an excellent time to hike the trail. Colorful wildflowers from trilliums and marsh marigolds to blue flag iris and wild geraniums carpet the area. In summer, the forest greenery dominates, but watch for trailside raspberries in July.

A variety of migrating songbirds also can be heard during spring. Squirrels, chipmunks, whitetailed deer and raccoon abound as well through summer and autumn.

Be sure to carry insect repellent, however, as mosquitoes, deerflies and horseflies sometimes can be an annoyance. Always check for deer ticks after returning from the trail. Also, make sure kids stay on the walking path, as poison ivy grows in the area (Remember: "Leaves of three, let it be.").

The handicap-accessible trail ends at a riverside campground. A primitive trail continues on but is not recommended for a day hike. Bathrooms, a playground, picnic area, and boat launch are located at Lion's Club Park.

Other St. Croix Falls Area Trails

■ **Esker Trail** – This short trail runs atop a tall ridge of sediment left by the meltwater of a retreating glacier that was last seen in these parts some 10,000 years ago. The ridge offers fantastic views of the St. Croix River with visibility of up to eight miles on clear days.

■ **Ladder Tank Trail** – At the scenic riverway visitor's center, you can take 60 stairs to the top of a ridge for an overlook of the St. Croix. It's a short trail but pretty with a great view at the top.

■ **Riegel Park Trail** – The west end of Wisconsin's Ice Age National Scenic Trail is part of this trail at the village's 76-acre Riegel Park Preserve. A trap rock meadow covered in moss and lichen with scattered trees blankets the preserve.

■ **Rock Creek Trail** – Located about five miles east of town, the trail parallels its namesake through a 20-acre restored prairie. Boulders on the forested part of the trail were brought here by glaciers.

Wild River State Park
River Terrace Loop

Day hikers can learn about the power of dams while enjoying a wooded walk along the St. Croix River on the River Terrace Loop in Minnesota's Wild River State Park.

The 1.5-mile loop and its stem trail circles through a bottomland forest in this popular park. Originally called St. Croix Wild River State Park – and it still appears on various maps that way – it's now just Wild River State Park.

Late summer and early fall mark the best time to hike the loop. During wet years, spring floods and mosquitoes can make the hike difficult.

To reach the trail, from North Branch, Minn., take Minn. Hwy. 95 to County Road 12. Drive County Road 12 to the park entrance, and follow the main park road to a parking lot near the picnic area.

The trailhead begins in the picnic area with a

short 0.1-mile connector that heads 120 feet down the bluff into the bottomlands and to the loop. Upon reaching the loop, go right/east.

In about 0.2 miles, you'll reach the St. Croix River and the Old Nevers Dam site. Wooden pilings in midstream are all that remain of the dam, which at one time was among the most important in the Midwest.

During the last half of the 1800s, log jams were a regular occurrence on the St. Croix as lumber cut in northern Wisconsin and Minnesota was floated downstream to sawmills. In 1886 when an estimated 150 million feet of lumber backed up on the river, loggers dynamited the tree trunks to break open the jam.

The solution to the log jams was controlling the river flow through a dam. To that end, in 1890, the Nevers Dam opened, virtually eliminating the backups. For the next 65 years, it held the record as the world's largest pile-driven dam.

As the lumberjacking days ended, Nevers Dam became a river control point that allowed construction of a hydroelectric power dam in St. Croix Falls, Wis., 11 miles downriver.

Spring floods in 1954 demolished Nevers Dam, however. That May, the high waters undermined the dam and washed several sections away. A wrecking crew removed what remained of the unusable dam in 1955.

From the Nevers Dam site, go left/north on the

trail, which parallels the river for 0.6 miles. Though wooded, during wet years this can be somewhat of a swampy area. Keep an eye out for ducks, herons and bitterns.

When the trail curves southwest and away from the river, you'll reach another junction. The intersecting trail accesses the campground atop the bluff via 164 winding steps.

The River Terrace loop goes left/south. Camper cabins are on the bluffs about 140 feet above.

As the bottomland forest sometimes is flooded during spring, inundation-tolerant trees – including silver maple and basswood – flourish here.

In 0.5 miles, the trail reaches another junction; go left/east and then within a few feet at the next intersection, go right/south back onto the connector trail leading to the picnic area and your parking lot.

Other Wild River State Park Trails

■ **Amador Prairie Loops** – Day hikers can choose between a 1-mile and a 2-mile loop that heads through an open area of tall prairie grasses. The loops begin at the park's Trail Center.

■ **Amik's Pond Trail** – Brochures for the nature trail can be picked up at its trailhead next to the visitor center. The walking path runs one mile.

■ **Deer Creek Loop** – Part of the pretty trail runs along the historic Old Military Road that once connected what is now the south end of the scenic riverway with Lake Superior. Including the stem trail from either the visitor center or the River Access, the trail runs four miles round trip.

■ **Mitigwaki Loop** – The 1-mile loop heads through an oak woods overlooking Dry Creek. The trailhead is at the visitor center.

■ **Pioneer Trail** – Day hikers can experience three ecosystems – on oak woods, a savanna, and a prairie – on this loop that leaves from the Trail Center. Including an access trail, the walk is 3.1-miles round trip.

■ **Windfall Trail** – Like the Amik's Pond Trail, a brochure for the nature trail is located at its visitor center trailhead. It is 1-mile long.

Grantsburg Area Trails
Sandrock Cliffs Trail

Unique, imposing bluffs set above a lush river await hikers of the Sandrock Cliffs Trail near Grantsburg, Wis. Up to five miles of trails run through the area in the scenic riverway along the state border.

The southernmost trail – a 3-mile loop – offers more than enough scenery, but connecting trails provide an additional two miles of hiking for visitors with a little more energy to burn.

To reach the Sandrock Cliffs Trail, take Wis. Hwy. 70 toward the St. Croix River. Before the bridge entering Minnesota, turn north into the

Hwy. 70 Landing parking lots.

The trailhead sits on the parking lot's north side. Go clockwise on Loop A, which heads north along the river. Paths are fairly well maintained. There are some hills along the way, but they're nothing elementary school kids or older can't handle.

The first section of the loop follows a terrace along the river through a forest of red and white pines. Peacefulness abounds as you walk across a soft and fragrant bed of pine needles.

River views also wow hikers on this trail. The St. Croix's clear, pristine water teems with smallmouth bass and freshwater mussels. This far north, the river channel is fairly shallow, so thin sandy islands, riffles and shoals are commonplace.

Watch overhead for patrolling eagles and ospreys. They nest nearby.

On the ground, look for a variety of woodland animals, most notably porcupines, ducks and deer. Ash, maple, jack pine and aspen as well as an understory of ferns grow amid the dominant red and white pines.

About halfway through Loop A, turn onto Loop E, continuing the walk clockwise (or paralleling the river). Along this 0.3-mile loop, you'll spot the highlight of the trail: picturesque sandstone cliffs towering over a river side channel.

Stand on the sandstone cliffs, and you're atop what once was the bottom of a shallow sea 500 million years ago. After the Cambrian-era sea evaporated, the sand deposits left behind were compressed into rock. Some 11,000 years ago during the end of the last ice age, raging flood waters carved out the riverway and exposed the sandstone.

The sandstone does give way easily, so remain clear of cliff edges. Also, carving or writing your name into the cliffs is illegal.

About halfway through Loop E, join Loop B for a 0.3-mile loop. Just a little bit onto Loop B are picnic tables perfect for lunch or a rest break with snack.

Bathrooms can be found about midway along Loop B. They're in the Tennessee Road parking lot.

Heading around the top curve of Loop B, its southern side rejoins Loop E, which in turn rejoins Loop A for a walk back to your parking lot near Hwy. 70.

This set of trails also can be accessed from its north side via Tennessee Road. Two additional trails – Loop C and Loop D, both 0.9 miles long – run north of Tennessee Road.

Dogs are allowed on all loops, so long as they remain leashed.

Governor Knowles State Forest
Cedar Interpretive Trail

You can see trees that are more than 200 years old on the Cedar Interpretive Trail in Governor Knowles State Forest.

To reach the trail, from Grantsburg take North Pine Street/County Road F north through Crex Meadows. In about seven miles, the road curves east. After the curve, turn left/north onto Norway Point Landing Road. Park in the lot before the road ends at Norway Point Landing. The trailhead is east of the parking lot.

You can't get lost on the trail, as the 1-mile round trip is on a boardwalk. It partially crosses the 330-acre Norway Point Bottomlands State Natural Area, which adjoins the state forest.

The trail is named for the stately eastern white cedar, which here are at their northern limit in Wisconsin. Cedars can live for up to 400 years; the cedars you pass that are a foot in diameter were mere saplings during the War of 1812.

The cedars sit in a floodplain forest. Though you'll only walk a half-mile one way, you'll head through an impressive five major lowland plant communities.

Among them is the Northern sedge meadow. Sedges and grasses dominate in depressions and the margins of nearby Iron Creek. This plant community occurs in several locations across northern and central Wisconsin.

The shrub carr ecosystem – tall shrubs, includeing meadowsweet, red-osier and silky dogwood, and willows – run through the forest. Though a common wetlands ecosystem in Wisconsin, it usually occurs farther south.

You'll know you're walking through the northern wet-mesic forest ecosystem once mosses, lichens, ferns and wildflowers dominate the forest floor. The mineral-enriched groundwater from seepages helps support these plants.

When maples, elms and ash trees with an open understory appear, you're heading through the southern wet-mesic forest community in the flood-plain. This is the northernmost reach of the ecosystem in Wisconsin.

The trail's end comes alongside Iron Creek, a minnow stream and tributary of the St. Croix River. The creek's waters generally are acidic and infertile.

Each of these plant communities are fragile ecosystems within the bottomlands, so don't step on or remove plants, many of which are rare.

Also, be forewarned that the boardwalk can be a bit uneven as roots break through the wood and as springs and seeps feed Iron Creek to the north. Because of this, you should wear waterproof hiking boots, even on the boardwalk. Insect repellent also is a good idea.

If you have a little extra energy, when the boardwalk ends, continue on the Kohler Peet Hiking Trail, a backcountry trail.

Other Governor Knowles State Forest Trails

■ **Benson Brook Hiking Trail** – A lengthy St.

Croix River trail at seven miles, the path can be accessed at three points: its terminus at the Rush City
Ferry Landing off of County Road O in the south;
close to its center at the northern tip of Pleasant
Prairie Road; or its terminus at West River Road in
the north.

■ **Brandt Pines Interpretive Trail** – The 2.5-
mile trail heads through a 130-year-old stand of
red and white pines near the St. Croix River in the
Brandt Pines State Natural Area. To reach the trail,
from Wis. Hwy. 70 west of Grantsburg, take Larson
Road north; it becomes Gile Road. Where the road
angles right/east at the junction with Hardwood
Ridge Trail, go left/west into the parking lot.

■ **Foxes Landing Trail** – From the parking lot at
Norway Point Road, the first two miles of this nine-
mile trail along the St. Croix River are particularly
scenic. Watch the skies for soaring bald eagles.

■ **Kohler Peet Hiking Trail** – The 6-mile trail
opens with the Cedar Interpretive Trail on its way
to the Clam Flowage. This jeep trail parallels an
old railbed.

■ **Lagoo Creek Hiking Trail** – The trail runs for
seven miles alongside the St. Croix River between
Evergreen Avenue in Polk County to County Road
O at the Rush City Ferry Landing. Parking is available at both ends of the trail.

■ **Raspberry Hiking Trail** – The 3-mile trail
rambles alongside the St. Croix River. Park in a lot
at the northwestern corner of West River Road. It

passes Raspberry Landing on the St. Croix north to the Wood River.

■ **Sioux Portage Trail** – The 6-mile trail heads from the Sioux Portage Group Campground south to the Clam River flowage. The trail parallels the St. Croix River, crossing a stream and a couple of roads along the way.

■ **Wood River Interpretive Trail** – The 0.8-mile trail runs from the St. Croix Campground to near the Wood River, a tributary of the St. Croix River. Reach the trailhead by taking River Road south of Hwy. 70 to the campground.

Chengwatana State Forest
Redhorse Creek Northern Loop

Some 120 years ago, loggers swept through northeast Minnesota, as they fed a young nation's growing need for lumber to build homes, make furniture, and lay rail beds. Hikers can see how that era altered the landscape on the Redhorse Creek Northern Loop in the Chengwatana State Forest.

Islands of upland boreal forest in a sea of brushland and marshes forms this state forest along the St. Croix River in Pine County. The Chengwatana offers primitive camping sites and has designated trails for off-road and all-terrain vehicles.

To reach the state forest, from Interstate 35 take the Beroun exit onto County Road 14. After 6.25

miles, turn south onto County Road 10/Evergreen Road. In a little more than three miles when County Road 10 and Evergreen Road split, turn left/south-east onto the gravel road (staying on Evergreen Road) then go left/east onto Chengwatana Forest Road. Watch for signs that make finding your way easy.

Where the Chengwatana Forest Road itself forks, go right/southeast. After crossing a stream, you'll come to a parking lot on the road's left side.

For the trailhead, follow the road you came in on south to a gate. On the other side of the gate, the trail is a stem leading to three stacked loops. Red-horse Creek is on the stem's left.

At the first trail junction, you've reached the northernmost of the stacked loops; it runs for just under two miles. Go left/northeast so you do the trail clockwise. The trail is largely forested with a few spots that open to meadows.

The state forest's name is an anglicized version of the Ojibwe word *zhingwaadena*, which means white-pine town. During the 1800s, eastern white pine was the dominant tree here. Then the area was heavily logged with the pine trunks floated down the St. Croix River to sawmills in Stillwater. The loop you're on comes near the St. Croix after about a mile of walking.

At the next fork, go right. If you go left, you can extend the trail by either a little more than a mile by adding the middle stacked loop or by a little more than two miles through combining the middle and southern loop, which also will go along more of the river.

Today, paper birch and bigtooth and quaking aspen have largely replaced the white pine. The old granddaddy of the forest still can be found here, though, along with balsam fir, burr oak, jack pine, red oak, red pine, tamarack, and white spruce.

Upon reaching the next trail junction, continue on your trail (that is, head west). If you accidentally turn, you'll end up on a segment of the trail shared by the middle and southern loops.

The state forest still is logged today, though it's controlled. The loop passes through a few areas in which companies have timber permits.

At the next fork, go right/north. You're now solely on the northernmost loops and curving toward the trailhead.

Keep a watch out for wildlife. You're likely to spot the footprints of, if not see, white-tailed deer, bear, beaver, mink, muskrat, ruffed grouse and turkey in the forest.

A number of other birds also can be spotted here, thanks to the marshes and rivers. Bald eagles, northern harriers, osprey, sandhill cranes, and warblers all call the Chengwatana home. In spring and autumn, migrating waterfowl can be seen here as well.

The next junction is the stem you took to enter

the loop. Go left onto the stem back to the parking lot.

Other Chengwatana State Forest Trails

■ **Matthew Lourey State Trail** – Previously known as the Minnesota-Wisconsin Boundary Trail or Willard Munger Trail East, the Lourey runs for several miles north-south through the forest. Tamarack and burr oak dominate the route, with wild turkeys, beavers, mink and muskrat along the way.

■ **Snake River Campground Trail** – About a mile-long trail runs south of the Snake River near the primitive campground site. The pathway runs between the Matthew Lourey State Trail and the St. Croix River with stem trails to the campground.

St. Croix State Park

Kettle River Highbanks to Observation Tower Route

Day hikers can walk to and climb to the top of a 100-foot fire tower at St. Croix State Park in Pine County, Minn.

An amazing 127-plus miles of hiking trails cross the state park's 34,000 acres. A combination of three of them (dubbed the Kettle River Highbanks to Observation Tower Route) marks a great 3.6-mile (7.2-miles round trip) route for physically fit families with a lot of energy.

To reach the park from Interstate 35, exit in

Hinckley, Minn., taking Minn. Hwy. 48 east. At County Road 22, turn south. In about five miles, you'll reach the park headquarters. From there, turn right/west onto St. John's Road. At the point the road turns to gravel, you have about a nine-mile drive. Your destination is the Kettle River Highlands, which offers limited parking.

From there, hike north paralleling the road you drove in on. You'll first pass the Chapel Grove, an impressive stand of red pines. In about 1.5 miles, the road forks. Go right/northeast.

In just under 1.1 miles, a trail bridge crosses Bear Creek. At the next fork, go left/west. You're now on the Matthew Lourey State Trail, which links the park to the Chengwatana, St. Croix and Ne-madji state forests.

In about 0.8 miles, head off the Matthew Lourey by turning left/south for the observation tower. You'll arrive at the tower in about a third of a mile.

The Civilian Conservation Corps constructed the tower in 1937. For the next 40-plus years, watch-men assigned to it scanned the surrounding forests for fires. No breaks or reading were allowed, and visitors were limited to 10-minute stays. The last watchman sat here in 1981, when aerial surveys became the preferred way to spot forest fires.

These days, you can stay in the tower as long as you like. Looking south from it, Bear Creek runs west to east immediately below. In the distance is the Kettle River, a State Wild and Scenic River, which flows southeast to the St. Croix.

After taking in the view, follow the trail back to your vehicle, or have someone meet you at the parking lot below the tower (True, you could have driven straight to the tower, but then there wouldn't have been any hiking, would there?).

Other St. Croix State Park Trails

■ **Matthew Lourey State Trail** – This trail runs for several miles roughly north to south through the park. A pleasant 2.3-mile segment heads from a trail center to Hay Creek.

■ **Park Headquarters to Lake Clayton Route** – From the park headquarters, head west for 2.5 miles for Lake Clayton Beach. Have one of the adults in the group pick you up after a day of swimming.

St. Croix State Forest

Gandy Dancer State Trail segment

Day hikers can walk across an old railroad bridge over the St. Croix River at the scenic riverway and the St. Croix State Forest on the Wisconsin-Minnesota border.

The Gandy Dancer Trail, which starts dozens of miles south of the state forest in St. Croix Falls, Wis., crosses the border into Minnesota at Danbury, Wis. The segment described in this entry is about 2-miles round trip.

In Danbury, parking for trail access is next to the walking route north of Wis. Hwy. 77 between Wis. Hwy. 35 and North Glass Street. From the lot, take the trail north.

You'll head through a forested area. The mix of trees near the riverfront yields a fantastic multi-colored leaf display in autumn.

An added bonus for autumn hikers: You'll probably spot a number of migrating waterfowl, including sandhill cranes. Also watch for bald eagles, osprey, northern harriers and hawks, all of which reside year-round in the area.

In about 0.4 miles, you'll reach the tranquil blue waters of the St. Croix River as you pass through the scenic riverway. Cross the old railroad trestle bridge into Minnesota. To the left is a canoe access point for the river.

In short order, you'll cross the invisible line into the St. Croix State Forest, a 42,105-acre spread along the Tamarack and St. Croix rivers. The trail continues through woodlands, mainly bigtooth and quaking aspen with islands of red oak and other various northern hardwood trees.

About 0.6 miles from the bridge, the trail reaches a pine barrens with a large gravel turnout. This marks a good spot to turn back.

The Gandy Dancer does continue on, so if you have a little extra energy, feel free to walk a bit farther. The trail ultimately runs for 30 miles through Minnesota before crossing back into Wisconsin south of Superior.

Be forewarned that the Minnesota side is an OHV (off-highway vehicle) trail, so keep an eye on children. Also, be sure to use insect repellent in spring and summer.

Other St. Croix State Forest Trails

■ **Lower Tamarack River Trail** – From County Road 173, take the Tamarack Forest Trail to the parking lot for the hiking trailhead. Walk south, paralleling the Lower Tamarack River; at the second trail junction, turn back for a roughly 4-mile round trip.

■ **Matthew Lourey State Trail, County Road 173 to Campground segment** – The Matthew Lourey runs north to south through the park. Consider parking at the trailhead along County Road 173 and taking it southwest through wetlands to the campground for 2-mile round trip.

■ **Matthew Lourey State Trail, Churchill Lake segment** – From the same parking lot along County Road 173, head north past Churchill Lake for a 3-mile round trip. The trail north of the lake enters wetlands.

Schoen/Louise Parks
Schoen/Louise Parks Jeep Trail

Day hikers can ramble down a jeep trail heading from the blufftops to the St. Croix River south of its headwaters in Douglas County, Wis.

During the river's first twenty or so miles downstream from the Saint Croix Flowage, there are few access points though all of it is located in the scenic riverway. Two exceptions are Louise Park and Schoen Park, located roughly east of Cloverton, Minn., and west of Gordon, Wis.

Schoen and Louise parks both offer a boat landing and spots to camp but not much in the way of hiking trails. However, between the two parks is a jeep trail that largely is in the scenic riverway. It's a 0.6-mile out-and-back trail (1.2-mile round trip) that will take you into the wilds of northern Wisconsin.

To reach the trailhead, from Cloverton head east on County Road 32; upon crossing the Wisconsin border, it becomes County Road T. From Gordon, take U.S. Hwy 52 south and turn right/west onto County Road T. Regardless of the direction you came, turn south onto Rocky Branch Road. After the turn off for Louise Park, take the next left/south onto an unnamed road (If you've passed the access road to Schoen Park, you've gone too far south.).

Park off of the jeep trail near the intersection. The elevation is about 1045 feet above sea level.

From there, the trail gradually descends through a hardwood forest. In autumn, it offers an array of fall leaf colors, including brilliant reds and oranges to bright yellow and pine greens.

After 0.3 miles, though, the trail becomes steeper as it crosses an intermittent stream and then nears the river bottoms at about 940 feet elevation. Notice how the trees species change, with the number of pine and silver maples increasing.

As the trail reaches the river bottom, you'll hear the rush of water over its rocky streambed. Boulders stick out of the shallow river in several spots along this stretch, especially about 400 feet upstream where they form a series of small rapids.

Return to the trailhead the way you came. Dogs are welcome but must be on leash. There are no facilities on the trail.

Buckley Creek Barrens State Natural Area

Buckley Creek Barrens Trail

Day hikers can truly get back to nature with a walk through a pine barrens near the northern reach of the scenic riverway.

The Buckley Creek Barrens Trail is an undesignated out-and-back footpath that runs 1.2-miles round trip through the Buckley Creek Barrens State Natural Area west of Gordon, Wis. Late summer and early autumn mark the best time to hike the trail, as spring through June will be wet and buggy.

To reach the trail, from U.S. Hwy. 53 in Gordon, head west on County Road Y. At about 4.4 miles, turn left/south onto South Lost Lake Road. After 4.3 miles, turn west onto Sunset Drive then in about a mile right/north onto Carp's Creek Road. The road runs north/south through the state natural area. In about 1.5 miles, you'll see a footpath on both sides of the road. Park on the shoulder here so other vehicles can pass.

Go east on the trail, which heads through Buckley Creek Barrens' higher elevations. The St. Croix River is a few miles to the east curving north.

In this region of Wisconsin, a number of wetlands and small lakes dot the landscape, surrounded by pine barrens – areas of sandy soil that support mainly pine and oak. The barrens once were the bottom of a glacial lake that existed at the end of the last ice age, some 10,000 years ago.

The trail is a biologist's dream, especially for those studying the rare pine barrens ecosystem. After years of preventing wildfires – which flora in a barrens depends upon to maintain their life cycle – one broke out in 1997. A barrens much like that which existed before white settlers came to the area more than a century before has returned, providing a living lab.

Beyond jack pine and hill's oak, among the trees that you might spot on the trail are black and pin cherry. The wetlands host a number of grasses.

Because of this flora, butterflies and birds literally flock to the pine barrens. Among four rare Wisconsin butterfly species you might spot here are the cobweb skipper, the dusted skipper, Henry's elfin, and the Gorgone checkerspot. For birds, a number of thrashers, warblers and sparrows call the natural area home, and you might even spot an osprey or bald eagle overhead.

After 0.6 miles, the trail reaches a wetland's southeast tip. This marks a good spot to turn back.

State natural areas in Wisconsin typically don't have public facilities, and Buckley Creek Barrens is no exception. If you truly want to get into the wilds, this is a great hike. Be sure to use insect repellent and wear pants and long sleeves when walking the trail.

On the drive back to Gordon along County Road Y, you'll pass the Saint Croix Flowage. This man-made lake is often mistaken as the St. Croix River's headwaters; it is not part of the scenic riverway.

Gordon Dam County Park
Gordon Flowage Campground Trail

Day hikers can explore the northernmost reaches of the scenic riverway on the Gordon Flowage Campground Trail.

The roughly 2-mile round trip is a jeep trail running through the woods bordering the river. The trail actually is unnamed, but for convenience's sake, I've christened it here after the campground where it begins. It's located in Douglas County's Gordon Dam County Park.

To reach the trailhead, from U.S. Hwy. 53 in Gordon, Wis., go west on County Road Y. Within a half-mile, you'll see a lake on your right/north. That's the Saint Croix Flowage. After about seven miles, the road dead ends. This is the northern edge of the scenic riverway. Park in the Gordon Flowage Campground lot at the end of the county road.

Begin the hike by walking to the dam that creates the flowage about 300 feet northeast of the lot. The river is left/west of the dam with the 2247-acre flowage to the right/east.

The flowage – a man-made lake to prevent river flooding – reaches 28 feet deep and is popular among fishermen. Largemouth bass, northern pike, and panfish are fairly abundant in the moderately clear water. Sometimes referred to as the Gordon-Saint Croix Flowage, it boasts 29 miles of meandering shoreline.

The flowage isn't the St. Croix River's headwaters. The river rushes into the lake's east end near Gordon after roughly paralleling Hwy. 53 from Upper St. Croix Lake near Solon Springs, Wis., farther north.

From the dam, head back to the parking lot and pick up the jeep trail at the end of County Road Y. The trail heads west, with a brief jog south, through a mixed hardwood and pine forest. It's a lovely walk during autumn with the leaves alight in reds, oranges, yellows and dark greens. You won't see the river from the trail, but you'll likely hear it flowing over the dam.

In about 0.95 miles, the trail junctions with the asphalt Mail Road (Some maps label it as "West Mail Road" and others as "South Mail Road."). This marks a good spot to turn around.

Brule River State Forest
Bois Brule-St. Croix River Historic Portage Trail

Day hikers can walk upon what ranks among Wisconsin's oldest hiking trails – dating to 1680 but probably used as far back as prehistoric times – at the St. Croix River's headwaters.

The Bois Brule-St. Croix River Historic Portage Trail runs 4.4-miles round trip from Upper St. Croix Lake to the Brule River. While not in the scenic riverway, it is part of Wisconsin's Brule River State Forest.

The trail can be a difficult hike through swampy territory so is best done by only adults or families with older teens. May through October mark the best time to hit the trail, but you'll need to bring bug spray for mosquitoes in spring and summer.

To reach the trailhead, from downtown Solon Springs, Wis., take County Road A north for about three miles, rounding the northern side of Upper St. Croix Lake. Watch for signs saying the North Country Trail is "1000 Feet Ahead", then turn into the boat landing where you can park. Across the road from the parking lot, take the trail heading right/northeast. The Brule Bog Boardwalk Trail heads left or directly north.

The historic portage trail is the same route cross-ed centuries ago by Daniel Greysolon Sieur duLhut (a French explorer who opened the way for fur traders in the 1680s), Pierre Lesueur (who estab-lished French stockades across this region in the 1690s), and Henry Schoolcraft (who found the source of the Mississippi River in the 1830s). His-torical markers on moss-lined boulders along the trail tell their stories as well as other significant white explorers.

They selected this portage because it was a quick link between the Great Lakes and the Miss-issippi River. Upper St. Croix Lake is the St. Croix River's headwaters while the spring-generated Brule River flows north into Lake Superior. It was the easiest way to traverse the continent from the Atlantic Ocean through the Great Lakes down the Mississippi River to the Gulf of Mexico...though for the marshy 2.2 miles between the Brule and Upper St. Croix, they would have to portage – or carry on foot – their boats and supplies.

As with so many of the early white explorers, Native Americans showed them the route. Local tribes had used the portage for millennia. Today, the Portage Trail is on the National Register of Historic Landmarks.

The portage was possible only because at the end of the last ice age some 10,000 years ago, a river flowed here from glacial Lake Superior, carving out a gorge and then the steep-sided valley. As the heavy glaciers retreated, the land rose in elevation, causing the river to dry up between the Brule and Upper St. Croix. The section that became the Brule reversed its course and now drops 420 feet over 44 miles from the portage to the Great Lake.

The trail is fairly narrow and at spots only shoulder-wide. It also is heavily forested with leaves covering much of the path. Wild blueberries grow alongside the trail.

There are some up and down climbs during the first mile as the trail parallels St. Croix Creek, which is on the left. Where the creek pools marks the St. Croix River's northernmost reach.

The out-and-back trail remains fairly flat to the Brule. After passing the Lesueur Stone, look on your left for the spring-fed creek that flows into the Brule. Upon reaching the river, turn back. The route is part of the North Country National Scenic Trail and continues north along the river.

Namekagon River Trails

Most day hiking trails along the Namekagon are located in clusters around the towns of Trego and Hayward, Wis., and in the Chequamegon National Forest east of Cable. Several access points to the river can be found along U.S. Hwy. 63 from Trego to south of Cable. A visitor center is located along that highway about a mile east of Trego.

Danbury Area Trails
Namekagon Delta Trail

Families can day hike to a scenic delta at the confluence of the St. Croix and Namekagon rivers on a trail in Wisconsin's Northwoods.

A number of unnamed and non-maintained trails run near the delta in the scenic riverway. For convenience sake, I've named this 2.7-mile out-and-back trail the Namekagon Delta Trail after its primary geographic feature.

Some of the area that the trail crosses, including the confluence itself, actually is part of the Big Island State Natural Area, but the boundaries with the scenic riverway are indistinguishable.

Like a wishbone, the scenic riverway splits in Burnett County, Wis. One fork – the St. Croix River – continues northward to its headwaters while the other fork – the Namekagon River – heads eastward.

To reach the trailhead, from Danbury, Wis., take Wis. Hwy. 35 north. Turn right/east onto the paved road named Springbrook Trail (If you've crossed the St. Croix River, you've just missed the turn.). Next, turn left/north onto Namekagon Point Road. The road stops at a vista of the Namekagon and St. Croix's confluence, which sits about 94 feet below. Park off to the side of the road.

Take the jeep trail that heads to the left/northwest. It quickly descends about 90 feet to the river valley, heading through a woods to the confluence for a half-mile.

The Namekagon Delta includes a sandbar that doesn't quite cut the St. Croix's width in half, but it does narrow the flow by diminishing the latter's depth. Only a hundred feet or so south of the delta, the St. Croix widens to the same distance as it was north of the confluence.

Heading back up the cliffside to the vista site, take the fairly flat primitive trail running southwest along the bluff line. Its trailhead is along Name-kagon Point Road just south of the vista.

The bluff line stretch of the trail runs for 0.85 miles one way, offering views of the confluence and then the St. Croix River in the tree breaks. The large island in the St. Croix's center is Big Island. Where the primitive trail reaches a jeep trail (listed on some maps as "Snowmobile Trail") marks a good turnaround point.

During spring into late summer, mosquito repellant is a necessity at the confluence.

Trego Area Trails

Trego Lake Trail

A pretty hike through a Northwoods forest awaits hikers on the Trego Lake Trail in the scenic river-way.

The 1.9-mile trail loops through the woods next to Trego Lake in Washburn County. Also known as

the Trego Lake Ski Touring Trail, the path described here is a segment of its various routes. Up
to 3.5 miles of trails are groomed here for cross
country skiing in winter.

To reach the trail, drive north of Trego, Wis., on
U.S. Hwy. 53. Go left/west on North River Road. In
two miles, turn left/south into a parking lot. Take
the stem trail from the lot's southern side to the
main trail, where you'll go left/east.

The trail parallels North River Road but is nicely
set inside a woodlands. In autumn, the trail is
comely with the yellow of birch trees leaves and
orange and browns of various oaks amid the mixed
hardwood and pine forest. You stand a good
chance of spotting white-tailed deer and ruffed
grouse in the woods.

Gradually the trail curves south then hairpins
west as coming to Trego Lake. The 383-acre water-
body actually is a widening of the Namekagon
River. As such, the lake isn't particularly deep,
reaching a maximum depth of just 36 feet.

About half of the trail follows the shoreline, including going onto a small peninsula. You're likely
to see fishermen on the lake, as they try to land
muskie, bass (both largemouth and smallmouth
flourish here), walleye, and various panfish. Northern pike and sturgeon also inhabit the lake.

After going beneath a powerline, the trail curves
north, then as nearing the road, parallels it as
turning east and passing under the powerline

again. Upon reaching the stem trail, go left/north back to the parking lot.

Since the trail described here is the outer loop of the ski trails, you can shorten the walk. After hiking a brief section of the shoreline, a trail goes right/ north and cuts across the woods to the parking lot. This shorter route totals 1.2 miles.

You also can extend it. After veering north away from the lake, take the next trail going right/north- east; this loops over hilly terrain and rejoins the trail proper, adding about a mile to the route for a 2.9-mile round trip. Upon rejoining the trail, go right/north back to the parking lot.

Dogs are welcomed on the trail, and restrooms can be found at the trailhead.

Trego Nature Trail

A pleasant walk through the woods along a wild river await hikers on the Trego Nature Trail in the scenic riverway.

The trail is best done during summer when the shaded walk keeps hikers cool. Early fall is a good time for those who enjoy fall colors.

To reach the trail, take U.S. Hwy. 63 north of Trego village. About 1.3 miles from the visitor cen- ter and after crossing the bridge over the Name- kagon River, take the first right.

The parking lot is at the end of this entrance road.

Look for the trailhead on the parking lot's east

side. The trail is fairly well-maintained. Watch for some steep inclines and narrow sections on curves, however.

The trail parallels the Namekagon River through a woods of pine and deciduous trees, with views of the waterway. Benches typically sit in the view-spots.

Hikers are likely to see a variety of wildlife or at least signs of it. White-tailed deer, turtles, fox, muskrat, bobcats, squirrels, snowshoe hares, and great blue heron abound in the riverway. Watch for otters and their slides, muddy paths cleared in the river's bank in which they move from land to water.

You also might spot lake sturgeon, Wisconsin's largest fish, especially if the water is low. They like to lay motionless beneath overhanging trees. In fact, the river's name comes from the Ojibwe Indian words that loosely mean "place of the sturgeon." Most of the sturgeon, however, are downriver below the Trego Dam.

After the footbridge, the trail loops back upon itself. Hikers can return to the parking lot the same way they came in. The trail comes to about 2.8 miles round trip.

Dogs are allowed on the trail if leashed. For safety, don't climb the river banks, as they can be slick.

On the drive back home, stop at the Namekagon Visitor Center for displays about the riverway.

Wild Rivers Trail segment

A tranquil stroll through the woods with a bridge view of the Namekagon River awaits day hikers on a segment of the Wild Rivers Trail in Trego.

At a little under 2.2-miles round trip, the segment is just a small portion of a trail that runs for 104 miles across three counties on an old Omaha and Soo Line Railroads rail line. The trail connects Rice Lake, Wis., in the south with Superior, Wis., to the northwest.

To pick up the trail in Trego, when U.S. Hwy. 53 enters the village from the south, turn right/east onto Oak Hill Road. Turn left/north onto Park Street. When Park Street curves west, you'll notice a large open gravel parking lot. Leave your vehicle there. The trail runs alongside the lot's eastern side.

Take the trail northeast. Nicely forested with typical northern hardwoods, the trail is fairly isolated from built-up areas.

This section of the trail also is part of the Ice Age National Scenic Trail. The 1200-mile Ice Age Trail essentially follows the edge of where the glacier last seen in these parts towered some 10,000 years ago.

In about a quarter mile, the trail begins to skirt the backside of the Namekagon Visitor Center grounds, which offers displays about the riverway. Unfortunately, there's no path leading from the Wild Rivers Trail to the center; when finished with the hike, consider a drive to it (take Hwy. 53 north and turn right onto U.S. Hwy. 63), especially if children are with you.

The trail then heads over busy Hwy. 63 and in another 100 feet crosses the Namekagon. From the river bridge looking west, the Namekagon breaks into a couple of back channels.

After the river, the trail re-enters the peaceful woods. You're likely to spot white-tailed deer, rabbits, squirrels and chipmunks along the way. Songbirds are plentiful, providing a sweet soundtrack to the hike. In 0.75 miles, the trail reaches Ross Road, which is a good spot to turn back; by this point, you've actually left the scenic riverway.

During spring and early summer, be sure to carry insect repellant when near the river. And while the trail cuts through woodlands, it is wide and mostly open, so also be also sure to don sunscreen.

Hayward Area Trails
Namekagon-Laccourt Oreilles Portage Trail

Though the Namekagon-Laccourt Oreilles Portage Trail memorializes a famous 18th century route where fur traders and explorers carried their canoes between rivers, hikers will head through a landscape much changed from that day. In fact, those fur traders and explorers probably wouldn't recognize the wild area.

Located near Hayward, Wis., in the scenic river-way, the modern trail is very close to the original portage route. A fur trader even operated a winter post during 1784 near the trail.

That portage route sprung up because travelers hoping to avoid problems with Sioux Indians near the St. Croix and Mississippi rivers junction de-cided to instead reach the continent's greatest wat-erway downstream from the Sioux by making a series of portages from the Namekagon to the Chippewa River, which joins the Mississippi at Lake Pepin.

To reach the portage trail, from Hayward go south on Wis. Hwy. 27. A historic marker erected in 1955 commemorates the portage. Turn left/west onto Rainbow Road then right/north onto Rolf Road. Upon entering the scenic riverway, take the first left/west. A parking lot will be on the right, and the trailhead begins there.

An easy, 0.8-mile loop, hikers will head through a second growth forest of mixed hardwoods and pines.

Those using the portage trail in the 1700s found quite different flora growing there.

At the time, this flat sandy area largely consisted of red and jack pines with white pines on the sur-rounding higher grounds. Most of that was logged off during the late 1800s, however, and the result is an area now dominated by maples, oaks, birch, red pine and spruce.

Logging and later small dams collaborated to change life in the Namekagon by leaving the shoreline open to sunlight. The result was an increase in the water temperature, which decimated some fish populations common during fur trading times.

At the loop's westernmost edge, hikers can take a short spur trail to the Namekagon, and it's well worth the walk, for the blue river is scenic. One thing the 101-mile long tributary to the St. Croix River does retain is its Ojibwa name, which means "at the place abundant with sturgeons." Today, bass, blacknose dace, brook trout, brown trout, cheek chub, Johnny Darter, mudminnow, northern pike, sculpin and sucker primarily live in the river. Rainbow Creek, which runs south of the trail and feeds the Namekagon, is a rainbow trout fishery.

Along the trail, hikers also can cross wetlands over a boardwalk. Watch and listen for bull frogs, turtles and waterfowl common in the area.

Cable Area Trails
Namekagon Dam Landing Trail

Day hikers can walk along the Namekagon River's headwaters on a trail in the scenic riverway's easternmost tip.

The 1.3-mile round trip walk is located in the southwest corner of the Chequamegon National Forest. June through September mark the best months to hike the trail.

To reach the trailhead, from Cable, Wis., take County Road M east. In about eight miles and after entering the national forest, turn left/north onto Dam Road/Forest Road 211. After crossing the Namekagon, take the first right, which heads to a small dam. A parking lot is located there.

The dam backs up the river into a flowage that heads east to Lake Namakagon (Note the different spelling from the river). The 2897-acre glacial lake in southern Bayfield County boasts 43.67 miles of shoreline. One of only three managed trophy muskie lakes in Wisconsin, it reaches a depth of 38 feet and even has islands.

From the dam, hike back up to Dam Road, go left, and walk alongside the asphalt back across the bridge. The bridge's corner offers a great view of the dam to the east and the narrow river to the west.

Continue walking south on Dam Road. About a thousand feet from the bridge, turn right/northwest onto Forest Road 1730. The jeep trail follows the top of the bluff overlooking the Namekagon. The bluff line runs anywhere from 20 to 40 feet higher than the river, which sits at a fairly even 1400 feet above sea level.

The trail heads beneath a canopy of mixed Northern hardwoods. During autumn, it makes for a fantastic display of golds and oranges accented with reds and dark evergreens.

The river below, nestled in a fen forest, is popular with canoeists and kayakers during summer. A series of small rapids sits about two miles below the dam; after the rapids, the river widens, and the fen forest gives way to open marsh.

On the bluff line trail, in about 350 feet from Dam Road, you'll cross a creek that flows into the Namekagon. Watch for beaver, which create ponds out of the stream and wetlands. Sometimes on the main river, beaver dams even will stop the paddlers.

In about 1000 feet from the creek, the trail ends at a high point of 1439 feet. From there, go back the way you came.

During early to mid-summer, be sure to carry insect repellant. Also, note that official maps do not call this the Namekagon Dam Landing Trail; the name is a convention for this book.

Best Trails List

Which trails are the best for seeing birds? Getting around on a wheelchair? Walking the family dog? Here are some lists of the best St. Croix National Scenic Riverway trails for those and many other specific interests.

Autumn leaves
- Namekagon Dam Landing Trail
- Riverside Trail
- South River Bluff Trail

Bridges
- Gandy Dancer Trail segment
- Wild Rivers Trail segment

Birdwatching
- Buckley Creek Barrens Trail
- Purple Trail
- Riverside Trail

Campgrounds
- Little Falls (Green) Trail
- River Terrace Loop
- Wood River Interpretive Trail

Dog-friendly
- Sandrock Cliffs Trail
- Schoen-Louise Parks Jeep Trail

Fire towers
- Kettle River Highbanks to Observation Tower Route

Geology
- Ridgeview Trail
- Shadow and Angle Rocks Lookout Trails
- Sandrock Cliffs Trail

Handicap accessible
- Hidden Ponds (Black) Nature Trail
- Indianhead Flowage Trail
- Riverside Trail

History/Archeology
- Bois Brule-St. Croix River Historic Trail
- Ridge View Trails
- River Terrace Loop

Minnesota
- North River Trail
- Riverside Trail
- Shadow and Angle Rocks Lookout Trails

Must-do's
- Riverside Trail

■ Summit Rock Trail
■ Trego Nature Trail

Picnicking
■ Lake O' the Dalles Trail
■ North River Trail
■ Sandrock Cliffs Trail

Plant communities
■ Buckley Creek Barrens Trail
■ Cedar Interpretative Trail
■ Ridgeview Trail

Swimming
■ Hidden Ponds Nature (Black) Trail
■ Lake O' the Dalles Trail
■ Park Headquarters to Lake Clayton Route

Vistas
■ Purple Trail
■ Shadow and Angle Rocks Lookout Trails
■ Summit Rock Trail

Waterfalls
■ Burkhardt (Pink) Trail
■ Cascade Falls Trail
■ Silverbrook Trail

Wildflowers
■ Hidden Ponds Nature (Black) Trail

- Indianhead Flowage Trail
- Ridgeview Trail

Wildlife
- Purple Trail
- Redhorse Creek Northern Loop
- Ridge View Trail

Wisconsin
- Summit Rock Trail
- Trego Nature Trail
- Burkhardt (Pink) Trail

Bonus Section: Day Hiking Primer

You'll get more out of a day hike if you research it and plan ahead. It's not enough to just pull over to the side of the road and hit a trail that you've never been on and have no idea where it goes. In fact, doing so invites disaster.

Instead, you should preselect a trail (This book's trail descriptions can help you do that). You'll also want to ensure that you have the proper clothing, equipment, navigational tools, first-aid kit, food and water. Knowing the rules of the trail and potential dangers along the way also are helpful. In this special section, we'll look at each of these topics to ensure you're fully prepared.

Selecting a trail

For your first few hikes, stick to short, well-known trails where you're likely to encounter others. Once you get a feel for hiking, your abilities, and your interests, expand to longer and more remote trails.

Always check to see what the weather will be like on the trail you plan to hike. While an adult might be able to withstand wind and a sprinkle here or there, if you bring children, for them it can be pure misery. Dry, pleasantly warm days with limited wind always are best when hiking with children.

Don't choose a trail that is any longer than the least fit person in your group can hike. Adults in good shape can go 8-12 miles a day; for kids, it's much less. There's no magical number.

When planning the hike, try to find a trail with a mid-point payoff – that is something you and definitely any children will find exciting about halfway through the hike. This will help keep up everyone's energy and enthusiasm up during the journey.

If you have children in your hiking party, consider a couple of additional points when selecting a trail.

Until children enter their late teens, they need to stick to trails rather than going off-trail hiking, which is known as bushwhacking. Children too easily can get lost when off trail. They also can easily get scratched and cut up or stumble across poisonous plants and dangerous animals.

Generally, kids will prefer a circular route to one that requires hiking back the way you came. A return on an out-and-back trail often feels anti-climatic, but you can beat that by mentioning features that all of you might want to take a closer look at.

Once you select a trail, it's time to plan for your

day hike. Doing so will save you a lot of grief – and potentially prevent an emergency – later on. You are, after all, entering the wilds, a place where help may not be readily available.

When planning your hike, follow these steps:

- Print a road map showing how to reach the parking lot near the trailhead. Outline the route with a transparent yellow highlighter and write out the directions.
- Print a satellite photo of the parking area and the trailhead. Mark the trailhead on the photo.
- Print a topo map of the trail. Outline the trail with the yellow highlighter. Note interesting features you want to see along the trail and the destination.
- If carrying GPS, program this information into your device.
- Make a timeline for your trip, listing: when you will leave home; when you will arrive at the trailhead; your turn-back time; when you will return for the cabin in your vehicle; and when you will arrive at your cabin.
- Estimate how much water and food you will need to bring based on the amount of time you plan to spend on the trail and in your vehicle. You'll need at least 2 pints of water per person for every hour on the trail.
- Fill out two copies of a hiker's safety form. Leave one in your vehicle.

■ Share all of this information with a respon-
sible person remaining in civilization, leaving a hiker's safety form with them. If they
do not hear from you within an hour of when
you plan to leave the trail in your vehicle,
they should contact authorities to report you
as possibly lost.

Clothing

Footwear

If your feet hurt, the hike is over, so getting the
right footwear is worth the time. Making sure the
footwear fits before hitting the trail also is worth it.
With children, if you've gone a few weeks without
hiking, that's plenty of time for feet to grow, and
they may have just outgrown their hiking boots.
Check out everyone's footwear a few days before
heading out on the hike. If it doesn't fit, replace it.

For flat, smooth, dry trails, sneakers and cross-
trainers are fine; but if you really want to head onto
less traveled roads or tackle areas that aren't typically dry, you'll need hiking boots. Once you start
doing any rocky or steep trails – and remember
that a trail you consider moderately steep needs to
be only half that angle for a child to consider it extremely steep – you'll want hiking boots, which offer rugged tread perfect for handling rough trails.

Socks

Socks serve two purposes: to wick sweat away

from skin and to provide cushioning. Cotton socks aren't very good for hiking, except in extremely dry environments, because they retain moisture that can result in blisters. Wool socks or liner socks work best. You'll want to look for three-season socks, also known as trekking socks. While a little thicker than summer socks, their extra cushioning generally prevents blisters. Also, make sure kids don't put on holey socks; that's just inviting blisters.

Layering

On all but the hot, dry days, when hiking you should wear multiple layers of clothing that provide various levels of protection against sweat, heat loss, wind and potentially rain. Layering works because the type of clothing you select for each stratum serves a different function, such as wicking moisture or shielding against wind. In addition, trapped air between each layer of clothing is warmed by your body heat. Layers also can be added or taken off as needed.

Generally, you need three layers. Closest to your skin is the wicking layer, which pulls perspiration away from the body and into the next layer, where it evaporates. Exertion from walking means you will sweat and generate heat, even if the weather is cold. The second layer is an insulation layer, which helps keep you warm. The last layer is a water-resistant shell that protects you from rain, wind, snow and sleet.

As the seasons and weather change, so does the type of clothing you select for each layer. The first layer ought to be a loose-fitting T-shirt in summer, but in winter and on other cold days you might opt for a long-sleeved moisture-wicking synthetic material, like polypropylene. During winter, the next layer probably also should cover the neck, which often is exposed to the elements. A turtleneck works fine, but preferably not one made of cotton. The third layer in winter, depending on the temperature, could be a wool sweater, a half-zippered long sleeved fleece jacket, or a fleece vest.

You might even add a fourth layer of a hooded parka with pockets, made of material that can block wind and resist water. Gloves or mittens as well as a hat also are necessary on cold days.

Headgear

Half of all body heat is lost through the head, hence the hiker's adage, "If your hands are cold, wear a hat." In cool, wet weather, wearing a hat is at least good for avoiding hypothermia, a potentially deadly condition in which heat loss occurs faster than the body can generate it. Children are more susceptible to hypothermia than adults.

Especially during summer, a hat with a wide brim is useful in keeping the sun out of your eyes. It's also nice should rain start to fall.

For young children, get a hat with a chin strap.

They like to play with their hats, which will fly off in a wind gust if not "fastened" some way to the child.

Sunglasses

Sunglasses are an absolute must when walking through open areas exposed to the sun and in winter when you can suffer from snow blindness. Look for 100% UV-protective shades, which provide the best screen.

Equipment

A couple of principles should guide your purchases. First, the longer and more complex the hike, the more equipment you'll need. Secondly, your general goal is to go light. Since you're on a day hike, the amount of gear you'll need is a fraction of what backpackers shown in magazines and catalogues usually carry. Indeed, the inclination of most day hikers is to not carry enough equipment. For the lightness issue, most gear today is made with titanium and siliconized nylon, ensuring it is sturdy yet light. While the list of what you need may look long, it won't weigh much.

Backpacks

Sometimes called daypacks (for day hikes or for kids), backpacks are essential to carry all of the essentials you need – snacks, first-aid kit, extra clothing.

For day hike purposes, you'll want to get yourself an internal frame, in which the frame giving the backpack its shape is inside the pack's fabric so it's not exposed to nature. Such frames usually are lightweight and comfortable. External frames have the frame outside the pack, so they are exposed to the elements. They are excellent for long hikes into the backcountry when you must carry heavy loads.

As kids get older, and especially after they've been hiking for a couple of years, they'll soon want a "real" backpack. Unfortunately, most backpacks for kids are overbuilt and too heavy. Even light ones that safely can hold up to 50 pounds are inane for most children.

When buying a daypack for your child, look for sternum straps, which help keep the strap on the shoulders. This is vital for prepubescent children as they do not have the broad shoulders that come with adolescence, meaning packs likely will slip off and onto their arms, making them uncomfortable and difficult to carry. Don't buy a backpack that a child will "grow into." Backpacks that don't fit well simply will lead to sore shoulder and back muscles and could result in poor posture.

Also, consider purchasing a daypack with a hydration system for kids. This will help ensure they drink a lot of water. More on this later when we get to canteens.

Before hitting the trail, always check your children's backpacks to make sure that they have not overloaded them. Kids think they need more than they really do. They also tend to overestimate their own ability to carry stuff. Sibling rivalries often lead to children to packing more than they should in their rucksacks, too. Don't let them overpack "to teach them a lesson," though, as it can damage bones and turn the hike into a bad experience.

A good rule of thumb is no more than 25 percent capacity. Most upper elementary school kids can carry only about 10 pounds for any short distance. Subtract the weight of the backpack, and that means only 4-5 pounds in the backpack. Overweight children will need to carry a little less than this or they'll quickly be out of breath.

Child carriers

If your child is an infant or toddler, you'll have to carry him. Until infants can hold their heads up, which usually doesn't happen until about four to six months of age, a front pack (like a Snugli or Baby Bjorn) is best. It keeps the infant close for warmth and balances out your backpack. At the same time, though, you must watch for baby overheating in a front pack, so you'll need to remove the infant from your body at rest stops.

Once children reach about 20 pounds, they typically can hold their heads up and sit on their own. At that point, you'll want a baby carrier (sometimes called a child carrier or baby backpack), which can transfer the infant's weight to your hips when you walk. You'll not only be comfortable, but your child will love it, too.

Look for a baby carrier that is sturdy yet light-weight. Your child is going to get heavier as time passes, so about the only way you can counteract this is to reduce the weight of the items you use to carry things. The carrier also should have adjust-ment points, as you don't want your child to out-grow the carrier too soon. A padded waist belt and padded shoulder straps are necessary for your comfort. The carrier should provide some kind of head and neck support if you're hauling an infant. It also should offer back support for children of all ages, and leg holes should be wide enough so there's no chafing. You want to be able to load your infant without help, so it should be stable enough to stand so when you take it off the child can sit in it for a moment while you get turned around. Stay away from baby carriers with only shoulder straps as you need the waist belt to help shift the child's weight to your hips for more com-fortable walking.

Fanny packs

Also known as a belt bag, a fanny pack is vir-tually a must for anyone with a baby carrier as you can't otherwise carry a backpack. If your signif-icant other is with you, he or she can carry the backpack, of course. Still, the fanny pack also is a good alternative to a backpack in hot weather, as it will reduce back sweat.

If you have only one or two kids on a hike, or if they also are old enough to carry daypacks, your fanny pack need not be large. A mid-size pouch can carry at least 200 cubic inches of supplies, which is more than enough to accommodate all the materials you need. A good fanny pack also has a place to hook canteens to it.

Canteens

Canteens or plastic bottles filled with water are vital for any hike, no matter how short the trail. You'll need to have enough of them to carry about two pints of water per person for every hour of hiking.

Trekking poles

Also known as walking poles or walking sticks, trekking poles are necessary for maintaining stability on uneven or wet surfaces and to help reduce fatigue. The latter makes them useful on even surfaces. By transferring weight to the arms, a trekking pole can reduce stress on knees and lower back, allowing you to maintain a better posture and to go farther.

If you're carrying a baby or toddler on your back, you'll primarily want a trekking pole to help you maintain your balance, even if on a flat surface, and to help absorb some of the impact of your step.

Graphite tips provide the best traction. A basket

just above the tip is a good idea so the stick doesn't sink into mud or sand. Angled cork handles are ergonomic and help absorb sweat from your hands so they don't blister. A strap on the handle to wrap around your hand is useful so the stick doesn't slip out. Telescopic poles are a good idea as you can adjust them as needed based on the terrain you're hiking and as kids grow to accommodate their height.

The pole also needs to be sturdy enough to handle rugged terrain, as you don't want a pole that bends when you press it to the ground. Spring-loaded shock absorbers help when heading down a steep incline but aren't necessary. Indeed, for a short walk across flat terrain, the right length stick is about all you need.

Carabiners

Carabiners are metal loops, vaguely shaped like a D, with a sprung or screwed gate. You'll find that hooking a couple of them to your backpack or fanny pack useful in many ways. For example, if you need to dig through a fanny pack, you can hook the strap of your trekking pole to it. Your hat, camera straps, first-aid kit, and a number of other objects also can connect to them. Hook carabiners to your fanny pack or backpack upon purchasing them, so you don't forget them when packing. Small carabiners with sprung gates are inexpensive, but they do have a limited life span of a couple of dozen hikes.

Navigational tools

Paper maps

Paper maps may sound passé in this age of GPS, but you'll find the variety and breadth of view they offer to be useful. During the planning process, a paper map (even if viewing it online), will be far superior to a GPS device. On the hike, you'll also want a backup to GPS. Or like many casual hikers, you may not own GPS at all, which makes paper maps indispensable.

Standard road maps (which includes printed guides and handmade trail maps) show highways and locations of cities and parks. Maps included in guidebooks, printed guides handed out at parks, and those that are hand-drawn tend to be designed like road maps, and often carry the same positives and negatives.

Topographical maps give contour lines and other important details for crossing a landscape. You'll find them invaluable on a hike into the wilds. The contour lines' shape and their spacing on a topo map show the form and steepness of a hill or bluff, unlike the standard road map and most brochures and hand-drawn trail maps. You'll also know if you're in a woods, which is marked in green, or in a clearing, which is marked in white. If you get lost, figuring out where you are and how to get to where you need to be will be much easier with such information.

Satellite photos offer a view from above that is rendered exactly as it would look from an airplane. Thanks to Google and other online services, you can get fairly detailed pictures of the landscape. Such pictures are an excellent resource when researching a hiking trail. Unfortunately, those pictures don't label what a feature is or what it's called, as would a topo map. Unless there's a stream, determining if a feature is a valley bottom or a ridgeline also can be difficult. Like topo maps, satellite photos (most of which were taken by old Russian spy satellites), can be out of date a few years.

GPS

By using satellites, the global positioning system can find your spot on the Earth to within 10 feet. With a GPS device, you can preprogram the trailhead location and mark key turns and landmarks as well as the hike's end point. This mobile map is a powerful technological tool that almost certainly ensures you won't get lost – so long as you've correctly programmed the information. GPS also can calculate travel time and act as a compass, a barometer and altimeter, making such devices virtually obsolete on a hike.

In remote areas, however, reception is spotty at best for GPS, rendering your mobile map worthless. A GPS device also runs on batteries, and there's always a chance they will go dead. Or you may drop your device, breaking it in the process. Their screens are small, and sometimes you need a large paper map to get a good sense of the natural landmarks around you.

Compass

Like a paper map, a compass is indispensable even if you use GPS. Should your GPS no longer function, the compass then can be used to tell you which direction you're heading. A protractor compass is best for hiking. Beneath the compass needle is a transparent base with lines to help your orient yourself. The compass often serves as a magnifying glass to help you make out map details. Most protractor compasses also come with a lanyard for easy carrying.

Food and water

Water

As water is the heaviest item you'll probably carry, there is a temptation to not take as much as one should. Don't skimp on the amount of water you bring, though; after all, it's the one supply your body most needs. It's always better to end up with extra water than returning to your vehicle dehydrated.

How much water should you take? Adults need at least a quart for every two hours hiking. Children need to drink about a quart every two hours of walking and more if the weather is hot or dry. To keep kids hydrated, have them drink at every rest stop.

Don't presume there will be water on the hiking trail. Most trails outside of urban areas lack such amenities. In addition, don't drink water from local streams, lakes, rivers or ponds. There's no way to tell if local water is safe or not. As soon as you have drunk half of your water supply, you should turn around for the vehicle.

Food

Among the many wonderful things about hiking is that snacking between meals isn't frowned upon. Unless going on an all-day hike in which you'll picnic along the way, you want to keep everyone in your hiking party fed, especially as hunger can lead to lethargic and discontented children. It'll also keep young kids from snacking on the local flora or dirt. Before hitting the trail, you'll want to repackage as much of the food as possible as products sold at grocery stores tend to come in bulky packages that take up space and add a little weight to your backpack. Place the food in resealable plastic bags.

Bring a variety of small snacks for rest stops. You don't want kids filling up on snacks, but you do need them to maintain their energy levels if they're walking or to ensure they don't turn fussy if riding in a baby carrier. Go for complex carbohydrates and proteins for maintaining energy. Good options include dried fruits, jerky, nuts, peanut butter, pre-pared energy bars, candy bars with a high protein content (nuts, peanut butter), crackers, raisins and trail mix (called "gorp"). A number of trail mix rec-ipes are available online (*hikeswithtykes.blogspot. com*); you and your children may want to try them out at home to see which ones you collectively like most.

Salty treats rehydrate better than sweet treats do. Chocolate and other sweets are fine if they're not all that's exclusively served, but remember they also tend to lead to thirst and to make sticky messes. Whichever snacks you choose, don't ex-periment with food on the trail. Bring what you know kids will like.

Give the first snack within a half-hour of leaving the trailhead or you risk children becoming tired and whiny from low energy levels. If kids start ask-ing for them every few steps even after having something to eat at the last rest stop, consider timing snacks to reaching a seeable landmark, such as, "We'll get out the trail mix when we reach that bend up ahead."

Milk for infants

If you have an infant or unweaned toddler with you, milk is as necessary as water. Children who only drink breastfed milk but don't have their mother on the hike require that you have breast-pumped milk in an insulated beverage container (such as a Thermos) that can keep it cool to avoid spoiling. Know how much the child drinks and at what frequency so you can bring enough. You'll also need to carry the child's bottle and feeding nipples. Bring enough extra water in your canteen so you can wash out the bottle after each feeding. A handkerchief can be used to dry bottles between feedings.

Don't forget the baby's pacifier. Make sure it has a string and hook on it so it connects to the baby's outfit and isn't lost.

What not to bring

Avoid soda and other caffeinated beverages, alcohol, and energy pills. The caffeine will dehydrate children as well as you. Alcohol has no place on the trail; you need your full faculties when making decisions and driving home. Energy pills essentially are a stimulant and like alcohol can lead to bad calls. If you're tired, get some sleep and hit the trail another day.

First-aid kit

After water, this is the most essential item you can carry.

A first-aid kit should include:

■ Adhesive bandages of various types and sizes, especially butterfly bandages (for younger kids, make sure they're colorful kid bandages)

■ Aloe vera

■ Anesthetic (such as Benzocaine)

■ Antacid (tablets)

■ Antibacterial (aka antibiotic) ointment (such as Neosporin or Bacitracin)

■ Anti-diarrheal tablets (for adults only, as giving this to a child is controversial)

■ Anti-itch cream or calamine lotion

■Antiseptics (such as hydrogen peroxide, iodine or Betadine, Mercuroclear, rubbing alcohol)

■ Baking soda

■ Breakable (or instant) ice packs

■ Cotton swabs

■ Disposable syringe (w/o needle)

■ Epipen (if children or adults have allergies)

■ Fingernail clippers (your multi-purpose tool might have this, and if so you can dispense with it)

■ Gauze bandage

■ Gauze compress pads (2x2 individually wrapped pad)

■ Hand sanitizer (use this in place of soap)

■ Liquid antihistamine (not Benadryl tablets, however, as children should take liquid not pills; be aware that liquid antihistamines may cause drowsiness)

■ Medical tape

■ Moisturizer containing an anti-inflammatory

■ Mole skin

■ Pain reliever (a.k.a. aspirin; for children's pain relief, use liquid acetaminophen such Tylenol or liquid ibuprofen; never give aspirin to a child

under 12)
- Poison ivy cream (for treatment)
- Poison ivy soap
- Powdered sports drinks mix or electrolyte additives
- Sling
- Snakebite kit
- Thermometer
- Tweezers (your multi-purpose tool may have this allowing you to dispense with it)
- Water purification tablets

If infants are with you, be sure to also carry teething ointment (such as Orajel) and diaper rash treatment.

Many of the items should be taken out of their store packaging to make placement in your fanny pack or backpack easier. In addition, small amounts of some items – such as baking soda and cotton swabs – can be placed inside re-sealable plastic bags, since you won't need the whole amount purchased.

Make sure the first-aid items are in a waterproof container. A re-sealable plastic zipper bag is perfectly fine. As the Upper Midwest is a humid climate, be sure to replace the adhesive bandages every couple of months, as they can deteriorate in the moistness. Also, check your first-aid kit every few trips and after any hike in which you've just used it, so that you can replace used components and to make sure medicines haven't expired.

If you have older elementary-age kids and teen-agers who've been trained in first aid, giving them a kit to carry as well as yourself is a good idea. Should they find themselves lost or if you cannot get to them for a few moments, the kids might need to provide very basic first aid to one another.

Hiking with children: Attitude adjustment

To enjoy hiking with kids, you'll first have to adopt your child's perspective. Simply put, we must learn to hike on our kids' schedules – even though they may not know that's what we're doing.

Compared to adults, kids can't walk as far, they can't walk as fast, and they will grow bored more quickly. Every step we take requires three for them. In addition, early walkers, up to 2 years of age, prefer to wander than to "hike." Preschool kids will start to walk the trail, but at a rate of only about a mile per hour. With stops, that can turn a three-mile hike into a four-hour journey. Kids also won't be able to hike as steep of trails as you or handle as inclement of weather as you might.

This all may sound limiting, especially to long-time backpackers used to racking up miles or bag-ging peaks on their hikes, but it's really not. While you may have to put off some backcountry and mountain climbing trips for a while, it also opens up to you a number of great short trails and nature hikes with spectacular sights that you may have otherwise skipped because they weren't challeng–

ing enough.

So sure, you'll have to make some compromises, but the payout is high. You're not personally on the hike to get a workout but to spend quality time with your children.

Family dog

Dogs are part of the family, and if you have children, they'll want to share the hiking experience with their pets. In turn, dogs will have a blast on the trail, some larger dogs can be used as Sherpas, and others will defend against threatening animals.

But there is a downside to dogs. Many will chase animals and so run the risk of getting lost or injured. Also, a doggy bag will have to be carried for dog pooh – yeah, it's natural, but also inconsiderate to leave for other hikers to smell and for their kids to step in. In addition, most dogs almost always will lose a battle against a threatening animal, so there's a price to be paid for your safety.

Many places where you'll hike solve the dilemma for you as dogs aren't allowed on their trails. Dogs are verboten on some Wisconsin and Minnesota state parks trails but usually permitted on those in national forests. Always check with the park ranger before heading to the trail.

If you can bring a dog, make sure it is well behaved and friendly to others. You don't need your dog biting another hiker while unnecessarily defending its family.

Rules of the trail

Ah, the woods or a wide open meadow, peaceful and quiet, not a single soul around for miles. Now you and your children can do whatever you want.

Not so fast.

Act like wild animals on a hike, and you'll destroy the very aspects of the wilds that make them so attractive. Act like wild animals, and you're likely to end up back in civilization, specifically an emergency room. And there are other people around. Just as you would wish them to treat you courteously, so you and your children should do the same for them.

Let's cover how to act civilized out in the wilds.

Minimize damage to your surroundings

When on the trail, follow the maxim of "Leave no trace." Obviously, you shouldn't toss litter on the ground, start rockslides, or pollute water supplies. How much is damage and how much is good-natured exploring is a gray area, of course. Most serious backpackers will say you should never pick up objects, break branches, throw rocks, pick flowers, and so on – the idea is not to disturb the environment at all.

Good luck getting a four-year-old to think like that. The good news is a four-year-old won't be able to throw around many rocks or break many branches.

Still, children from their first hike into the wilderness should be taught to respect nature and to not destroy their environment. While you might overlook a preschooler hurling rocks into a puddle, they can be taught to sniff rather than pick flowers. As they grow older, you can teach them the value of leaving the rock alone. Regardless of age, don't allow children to write on boulders or carve into trees.

Many hikers split over picking berries. To strictly abide by the "minimize damage" principle, you wouldn't pick any berries at all. Kids, however, are likely to find great pleasure in eating black-berries, currants, and thimbleberries as ambling down the trail. Personally, I don't see any problem enjoying a few berries if the long-term payoff is a respect and love for nature. To minimize damage, teach them to only pick berries they can reach from the trail so they don't trample plants or deplete food supplies for animals. They also should only pick what they'll eat.

Collecting is another issue. In national and most state and county parks, taking rocks, flower blossoms and even pine cones is illegal. Picking flowers moves many species, especially if they are rare and native, one step closer to extinction. Archeological ruins are extremely fragile, and even touching them can damage a site.

But on many trails, especially gem trails, collecting is part of the adventure. Use common sense – if the point of the trail is to find materials to collect, such as a gem trail, take judiciously, meaning don't overcollect. Otherwise, leave it there.

Sometimes the trail crosses private land. If so, walking around fields, not through them, always is best or you could damage a farmer's crops.

Pack out what you pack in

Set the example as a parent: Don't litter yourself; whenever stopping, pick up whatever you've dropped; and always require kids to pick up after themselves when they litter. In the spirit of "Leave no trace," try to leave the trail cleaner than you found it, so if you come across litter that's safe to pick up, do so and bring it back to a trash bin in civilization. Given this, you may want to bring a plastic bag to carry out garbage.

Picking up litter doesn't just mean gum and candy wrappers but also some organic materials that take a long time to decompose and aren't likely to be part of the natural environment you're hiking. In particular, these include peanut shells, orange peelings, and eggshells.

Burying litter, by the way, isn't viable. Either animals or erosion soon will dig it up, leaving it scattered around the trail and woods.

Stay on the trail

Hiking off trail means potentially damaging fragile growth. Following this rule not only ensures you minimize damage but is also a matter of safety. Off trail is where kids most likely will encounter dangerous animals and poisonous plants. Not being able to see where they're stepping also increases the likelihood of falling and injuring themselves. Leaving the trail raises the chances of getting lost. Staying on the trail also means staying out of caves, mines or abandoned structures you may encounter. They are usually dangerous places.

Finally, never let children take a shortcut on a switchback trail. Besides putting them on steep ground upon which they could slip, their impatient act will cause the switchback to erode.

Trail dangers

On scenic riverway trails, two common dangers face hikers: ticks and poison ivy/sumac. Both can make your stay at the cabin or your time once back home miserable. Fortunately, both threats are easily avoidable and treatable.

Ticks

One of the greatest dangers comes from the smallest of creatures: ticks. Both the wood and the deer tick are common in the state and can infect people with Lyme disease and much more rarely Rocky Mountain spotted fever.

Ticks usually leap onto people from the top of a grass blade as you brush against it, so walking in the middle of the trail away from high plants is a good idea. Wearing a hat, a long sleeve shirt tucked into pants, and pants tucked into shoes or socks, also will keep ticks off you, though this is not foolproof as they sometimes can hook onto clothing. A tightly woven cloth provides the best protection, however. Children can pick up a tick that has hitchhiked onto the family dog, so outfit Rover and Queenie with a tick-repelling collar.

After hiking into an area where ticks live, you'll want to examine your children's bodies (as well as your own) for them. Check warm, moist areas of the skin, such as under the arms, the groin and head hair. Wearing light-colored clothing helps make the tiny tick easier to spot.

To get rid of a tick that has bitten your child, drip either disinfectant or rubbing alcohol on the bug, so it will loosen its grip. Grip the tick close to its head, slowly pulling it away from the skin. This hopefully will prevent it from releasing saliva that spreads disease. Rather than kill the tick, keep it in a plastic bag so that medical professionals can analyze it should disease symptoms appear. Next, wash the bite area with soap and water then apply antiseptic.

In the days after leaving the woods, also check for signs of disease from ticks. Look for bulls-eye rings, a sign of a Lyme disease. Other symptoms include a large red rash, joint pain, and flu-like symptoms. Indications of Rocky Mountain spotted fever include headache, fever, severe muscle aches, and a spotty rash first on palms and feet soles that spread, all beginning about two days after the bite.

If any of these symptoms appear, seek medical attention immediately. Fortunately, antibiotics exist to cure most tick-related diseases.

Poison ivy/sumac

Often the greatest danger in the wilds isn't our own clumsiness or foolhardiness but various plants we encounter. The good news is that we mostly have to force the encounter with flora. Touching the leaves of either poison ivy or poison sumac in particular results in an itchy, painful rash. Each plant's sticky resin, which causes the reaction, clings to clothing and hair, so you may not have "touched" a leaf, but once your hand runs against the resin on shirt or jeans, you'll probably get the rash.

To avoid touching these plants, you'll need to be able to identify each one. Remember the "Leaves of three, let it be" rule for poison ivy. Besides groups of three leaflets, poison ivy has shiny green leaves that are red in spring and fall. Poison sumac's leaves are not toothed as are non-poisonous sumac, and in autumn their leaves turn scarlet. Be forewarned that even after leaves fall off, poison oak's stems can carry some of the itchy resin.

By staying on the trail and walking down its middle rather than the edges, you are unlikely to come into contact with this pair of irritating plants. That probably is the best preventative. Poison ivy barrier creams also can be helpful, but they only temporarily block the resin. This lulls you into a false sense of safety, and so you may not bother to watch for poison ivy.

To treat poison ivy/sumac, wash the part of the body that has touched the plant with poison ivy soap and cold water. This will erode the oily resin, so it'll be easier to rinse off. If you don't have any of this special soap, plain soap sometimes will work if used within a half-hour of touching the plant. Apply a poison ivy cream and get medical attention immediately. Wearing gloves, remove any clothing (including shoes) that has touched the plants, washing them and the worn gloves right away.

For more about these topics and many others, pick up this author's "Hikes with Tykes: A Practical Guide to Day Hiking with Kids." You also can find tips online at the author's "Hikes with Tykes" blog (*hikeswithtykes.blogspot.com*). Have fun on the trail!

Index

A

Afton, 4, 6, 9, 19-21
Afton State Park, 6, 19-22
Amador Prairie Loops, 53
Amik's Pond Trail, 53-4

B

Backpacks 99-101, 104,
  112
Bayport, 4
Bear Creek, 64
Beaver Lodge Trail, 33
Belt bag, see *fanny packs*
Benson Brook Hiking
  Trail, 58-9
Beroun, 6, 60
Big Island State Natural
  Area, 78-9
Blue Trail, 18
Bois Brule-St. Croix River
  Historic Portage Trail,
  73-5, 90
Brandt Pines Interpretive
  Trail, 59
Brandt Pines State
  Natural Area, 59
Brown's Creek, 28
Brown's Creek Park and
  Nature Preserve, 27-9
Brown's Creek Park and
  Nature Preserve Ski
  Trail, 27-9

Brown Trail, 18
Brule Bog Boardwalk
  Trail, 74
Brule River, 73
Brule River State Forest,
  6, 73-5
Buckley Creek Barrens
  State Natural Area, 69-
  71, 89
Buckley Creek Barrens
  Trail, 69-71, 91
Burkhardt (Pink) Trail,
  24-6, 91-2
Bushwhacking, 94

C

Cable, 6, 9, 10, 77, 86-8
Canteens, 103
Carabiners, 104-5
Carpenter St. Croix
  Valley Nature Center, 6,
  12-4
Cascade Falls, 34-6
Cascade Falls Trail, 34-6
Cedar Interpretive Trail,
  56-8, 91
Chengwatana State
  Forest, 6, 60-4
Chequamegon National
  Forest, 5, 6, 77, 86
Child carriers, 101-2
Churchill Lake, 67

Clothing, 96-9
Cloverton, 68
Compass, 107

D
Dalles Creek, 44
Danbury, 4, 9, 11, 65-6,
    78-9
Daypacks, 99, 103
Deer Creek Loop, 53-4
Deer Valley Loop, 21
Dogs, 90, 104-5, 119
Dresser, 4

E
Eagle Peak Trail, 45
Eau Claire, 9
Echo Canyon Trail, 43
Equipment, 99-105
Esker Trail, 50

F
Fanny packs, 102-4, 112
First-aid kit, 110-13
Food, 95, 107-10
Footwear, 96
Foxes Landing Trail, 59
Front pack, 101

G
Gandy Dancer State Trail,
    65-7, 89
Geiger Falls, 35-6
Gordon, 4, 6, 68-9, 71
Gordon Dam County
    Park, 6, 71-3
Gordon Flowage
    Campground Trail, 71-3
Governor Knowles State

Forest, 6, 56-60
GPS, 95, 105-7
Grantsburg, 6, 9, 54-6, 59
Green Trail, 18-9

H
Hardwood Hills Trail, 33-
    4
Hastings, 6, 14-5
Hay Creek, 65
Hayward, 5, 9, 84-6
Headgear, 98-9
Hidden Ponds Nature
    (Black) Trail, 22-4, 90-1
Hydration system, 100
Hiker's safety form, 95-6
Hiking with children
    attitude, 113-14
Hinckley, 6, 9, 64
Horizon Rock Trail, 43
Hudson, 4-6, 9, 22
Hydration system, 100

I
Ice Age National Scenic
    Trail, 45, 49-51, 83
Indianhead Flowage
    Trail, 49-50, 90, 92
Iron Creek, 57-8

J
Junior Park Naturalist
    patches/certificates, 7
Junior Ranger Program, 7

K
Kettle River, 64-5
Kettle River Highbanks to
    Observation Tower

Route, 63-5, 90
Kinnickinnic River, 15-9
Kinnickinnic State Park,
  6, 15-9
Knapweed (Orange)
  Trail, 26
Kohler Peet Hiking Trail,
  58-9

L
Ladder Tank Trail, 50
Lagoo Creek Hiking
  Trail, 59
Lake Alice, 31-2
Lake O' the Dalles, 41,
  43-5
Lake O' the Dalles Trail,
  41, 43-5, 91
Lake St. Croix, 4, 20-1
Layering, 97-8
Leave no trace, 115-16
Lions Club Park, 49
Little Falls (Green) Trail,
  26, 89
Little Falls Lake, 24-6
Lost Pothole Trail, 47
Louise Park, 67-9
Lower Tamarack River
  Trail, 67

M
Maps, 95, 105-7
Marine on St. Croix, 4-6,
  29, 31, 33
Mathew Lourey State
  Trail, 63-5, 67
Minnesota Interstate State
  Park, 4, 6, 46-9
Minnesota-Wisconsin

Boundary Trail, see
  *Mathew Lourey State
  Trail*
Milk, 109-10
Mississippi River, 2, 3,
  13, 20, 74
Mitigawki Loop, 54
Mound (White) Trail, 26

N
Namakagon Lake, 5
Namekagon Dam
  Landing Trail, 86-9
Namekagon Delta Trail,
  78-9
Namekagon-Laccourt
  Oreilles Portage Trail,
  84-6
Namekagon River Visitor
  Center, 5
Navigational tools, 105-7
Nelson Farm (Silver)
  Trail, 26
Nemadji State Forest, 64
North Branch, 6, 51
North Country National
  Scenic Trail, 75
North Hudson, 4
North River Trail, 19-21,
  90-1
Norway Point
  Bottomlands State
  Natural Area, 57

O
Oak Park Heights, 4
Oak Ridge (Brown) Trail,
  26
O'Brien Trail North, 31

Old Man of the Dalles, 42
Orange Trail, 17-9
Osceola, 4, 6, 9, 34-41, 46
Osceola Bedrock Glades
   State Natural Area, 6, 36,
   38-41
Osceola Creek, 35-6
Osceola State Fish
   Hatchery, 36

P

Pack out what you pack
   in, 117
Park Explorer patches, 7
Park Headquarters to
   Lake Clayton Route, 65,
   91
Picnic Area Loop, 48
Pioneer Trail, 54
Pioneer (Yellow) Trail, 27
Poison ivy, 112, 120-21
Poison sumac, 120-21
Pothole Trail, 45-6
Prairie Loop, 21-2
Prairie Overlook Trail, 34
Prescott, 3, 6, 9, 11, 13,
   16, 20
Project Learning Tree, 7
Purple Trail, 15-8, 89, 91-
   2

R

Rainbow Creek, 86
Railroad Bed Trail, 13
Railroad Trail, 48
Raspberry Hiking Trail,
   59-60
Ravine Trail, 46

Redhorse Creek
   Northern Trail, 60-3, 92
Red Trail, 18
Rice Lake, 83
Ridge View (Osceola and
   Chisago) Trails, 36-8,
   89, 92
Ridgeview Trail, 36, 38-
   41, 90-2
Riegel Park Preserve, 51
Riegel Park Trail, 50-1
River Bluff Trail, 44
Riverside Trail, 30-2, 88-
   90
River Terrace Loop, 51-3,
   89-90
River Trail, 47-8
Rock Creek Trail, 51
Rolling Hills Savanna
   Trail, 34
Rules of the Trail, 115-18

S

St. Croix Bluffs Regional
   Park, 6, 14-5
St. Croix Bluffs Trail, 14-5
St. Croix Boom Site Trail,
   29-30
St. Croix Creek, 75
St. Croix Falls, 5, 6, 9, 11,
   41, 46, 49-52, 65
St. Croix O' the Dalles, 4
St. Croix River Visitor
   Center, 5
St. Croix State Forest, 6,
   64-7
St. Croix State Park, 6,
   63-5

St. Croix Wild River State
Park, see *Wild River
State Park*
St. Paul, 23
Saint Croix Flowage, 4,
68, 71-2
Sandrock Cliffs Trail, 54-
6, 90-1
Sandstone, 6
Sandstone Bluff Trail, 48-
9
Schoen Park 67-9
Schoen/Louse Parks Jeep
Trail, 67-9, 90
Selecting a trail, 93-6
Shadow and Angle Rocks
Lookout Trail, 46-8, 90-1
Silverbrook Falls, 46
Silverbrook Trail, 46, 91
Sioux Portage Trail, 60
Skyline Nature Trail, 46
Skyline Trail, 46
Snake River
Campground Trail, 63
Socks, 96-7
Solon Springs, 6, 11, 72-3
South River Bluff Trail, 12-
14, 89
South River Trail 22
Stay on the trail, 117-19
Stillwater, 4, 9, 20, 27-30
Summit Rock Trail, 41-3,
91-2
Sunglasses, 99
Superior, 67, 83

T

Tamarack River, 66

Taylors Falls, 3, 4, 6, 9, 48
Ticks, 118-20
Trail dangers, 118-21
Trail mix, 109
Trego, 5, 9, 77, 79-84
Trego Lake Ski Touring
Trail, 80
Trego Lake Trail, 79-81
Trego Nature Trail, 81-2,
91-2
Trout Brook Loop, 22
Trout Brook (Purple)
Trail, 26-7
Trekking poles, 103-4

U

Upper St. Croix Lake, 4,
72, 74

W

Walking poles, see
trekking poles
Walking stick, see
trekking poles
Water, 95, 100, 103, 107-
8
Weather, 93-4
Wedge Hill Savanna
Trail, 32-3
Wetland Trail, 33
Wild River State Park, 6,
51-4
Wild Rivers Trail, 83-4,
89
Willard Munger Trail
East, see *Mathew Lourey
State Trail*
William O'Brien State

Park, 4-6, 30-4
Willow Falls, 27
Willow River, 22, 26
Willow River Falls, 25
Willow River State Park,
 4, 6, 22-7
Windfall Trail, 54
Wisconsin Explorer
 patches, 8
Wisconsin Interstate State

Park, 4, 6, 41-6
Wisconsin Wildcards, 8
Woodland Edge Trail, 33-
 4
Wood River Interpretive
 Trail, 60, 89

Y
Yellow Trail, 15, 17-9

About the Author

Rob Bignell is a long-time hiker, journalist, and author of the popular "Hikes with Tykes" guidebooks and several other titles. He and his son Kieran have been hiking together for the past six years. Before Kieran, Rob served as an infantryman in the Army National Guard and taught middle school students in New Mexico and Wisconsin. His newspaper work has won several national and state journalism awards, from editorial writing to sports reporting. In 2001, The Prescott Journal, which he served as managing editor of, was named Wisconsin's Weekly Newspaper of the Year. Rob and Kieran live in western Wisconsin.

CHECK OUT THESE OTHER HIKING BOOKS BY ROB BIGNELL

"Headin' to the Cabin" series:
- Day Hiking Trails of Northeast Minnesota
- Day Hiking Trails of Northwest Wisconsin

"Hikes with Tykes" series:
- Hikes with Tykes: A Practical Guide to Day Hiking with Children
- Hikes with Tykes: Games and Activities

"Hittin' the Trail" ebooks:
- Barron County, Wis.
- Burnett County, Wis.
- Crex Meadow Wildlife Area (Wis.)
- Grand Canyon National Park
- Interstate State Park (Minn./Wis.)
- Polk County, Wis.

ORDER THEM ONLINE AT:
hikeswithtykes.com/hittinthetrail_home.html

WANT MORE INFO ABOUT FAMILY DAY HIKES?

Follow this book's blog, where you'll find:

Tips on day hiking with kids

Lists of great trails to hike with children

Parents' questions about
day hiking answered

Product reviews

Games and activities for the trail

News about the book series
and author

Visit online at:
hikeswithtykes.blogspot.com

www.ingramcontent.com/pod-product-compliance
Lightning Source LLC
Chambersburg PA
CBHW050351280326
41933CB00010BA/1412